"When people ask me which books have most marked my life and ministry, I never fail to mention *The Holiness of God*—its effect on me has been revolutionary. And the message of this book has never been more needed. If we fail to grasp God's holy character, we will never know God truly, we will never understand ourselves accurately, and we will never comprehend the significance of the cross. On such a critical truth, we need biblical clarity and appropriate solemnity, both of which mark this classic work by my friend R. C. Sproul."
— **C. J. Mahaney**, Sovereign Grace Ministries

"In a culture saturated with self, Christians desperately need to recover a biblical vision of the greatness and glory of God. God used this book to focus that vision in my life. Buy it, read it, and He will do the same for you."
— **Pastor Colin Smith**, Senior pastor, The Orchard Evangelical Free Church and president of *Unlocking the Bible* broadcast

THE HOLINESS OF GOD

RC SPROUL

Tyndale House Publishers, Inc.
Carol Stream, Illinois

Visit Tyndale's exciting Web sites at www.newlivingtranslation.com and www.tyndale.com.

TYNDALE and Tyndale's quill logo are registered trademarks of Tyndale House Publishers, Inc.

The Holiness of God

Copyright © 1985, 1998 by R. C. Sproul. All rights reserved.

First edition 1985

Second edition 1998

All Scripture quotations, unless otherwise indicated, are taken from the Holy Bible, *New International Version.*® *NIV.*® Copyright © 1973, 1978, 1984 by Biblica, Inc.™ Used by permission of Zondervan. All rights reserved worldwide.

Scripture quotations marked KJV are taken from *The Holy Bible,* King James Version.

Scripture quotations marked NASB are taken from the New American Standard Bible® copyright © 1960, 1962, 1963, 1968, 1971, 1972, 1973, 1975, 1977, 1995 by The Lockman Foundation. Used by permission.

Scripture quotations marked NKJV are taken from the New King James Version®. Copyright © 1982 by Thomas Nelson, Inc. Used by permission. All rights reserved. *NKJV* is a trademark of Thomas Nelson, Inc.

ISBN 978-1-4143-3790-6 (Man in the Mirror ed.)

Printed in the United States of America

16   15   14   13   12   11   10
07   06   05   04   03   02   01

*To Kaki and Ryan
and to their generation,
that they may live during
a new reformation*

CONTENTS

ACKNOWLEDGMENTS

My special thanks go to Wendell Hawley for his warm and kind encouragement in this project. If the book has any clarity, the credit must go to my wife, Vesta, who is my most ruthless and loving editor.

The Holy Grail

Gaily bedight, a gallant knight
In sunshine and in shadow;
Riding along, singing a song,
In search of El Dorado.

EDGAR ALLEN POE

I was compelled to leave the room. A deep, undeniable summons disturbed my sleep; something holy called me. The only sound was the rhythmic ticking of the clock on my desk. It seemed vague and unreal, as if it were in a chamber, submerged under fathoms of water. I had reached the beginning edge of slumber, where the line between consciousness and unconsciousness is blurred. I was suspended in that moment when one hangs precariously on the edge, a moment when sounds from the outside world still intrude on the quietness of one's brain, that moment just before surrender to the night occurs. Asleep, but not yet asleep. Awake, but not alert. Still vulnerable to the inner summons that said, "Get up. Get out of this room."

The summons became stronger, more urgent, impossible to ignore. A burst of wakefulness made me jerk upright and swing my legs over the side of the bed and onto the floor. Sleep vanished in an instant, and my body sprang into resolute action. Within seconds I was dressed and on the way out of my college dormitory. A quick glance at the clock registered the time in my mind. Ten minutes before midnight.

The night air was cold, turning the snow of the morning to a hard-crusted blanket. I felt the crunch under my feet as I walked toward the center of campus. The moon cast a ghostly pall on the college buildings, whose gutters were adorned with giant icicles—dripping water arrested in space, solid daggers of ice that resembled frozen fangs. No human architect could design these gargoyles of nature.

The gears of the clock atop Old Main Tower began to grind, and the arms met and embraced vertically. I heard the dull groan of the machinery a split second before the chimes began to ring. Four musical tones signaled the full hour. They were followed by the steady, sonorous striking of twelve. I counted them in my mind, as I always did, checking for a possible error in their number. But they never missed. Exactly twelve strokes pealed from the tower like an angry judge's gavel banging on metal.

The chapel was in the shadow of Old Main Tower. The door was made of heavy oak with a Gothic arch. I swung it open and entered the narthex. The door fell shut behind me with a clanging sound that reverberated from the stone walls of the nave.

The echo startled me. It was a strange contrast to the sounds of daily chapel services, where the opening and closing of the doors were muffled by the sounds of students shuffling to their assigned places. Now the sound of the door was amplified into the void of midnight.

I waited for a moment in the narthex, allowing my eyes a few seconds to adjust to the darkness. The faint glow of the moon seeped through the muted stained-glass windows. I could make out the outline of the pews and the center aisle that led to the chancel steps. I felt a majestic sense of space, accented by the vaulted arches of the ceiling. They seemed to draw my soul upward, a sense of height that evoked a feeling of a giant hand reaching down to pick me up.

I moved slowly and deliberately toward the chancel steps. The sound of my shoes against the stone floor evoked terror-filled images of German soldiers marching in hobnailed boots along cobblestone streets. Each step resounded down the center aisle as I reached the carpet-covered chancel.

There I sank to my knees. I had reached my destination. I was ready to meet the source of the summons that had disturbed my rest.

I was in a posture of prayer, but I had nothing to say. I knelt there quietly, allowing the sense of the presence of a holy God to fill me. The beat of my heart was telltale, a *thump-thump* against my chest. An icy chill started at the base of my spine and crept up my neck. Fear swept over me. I fought the impulse to run from the foreboding presence that gripped me.

The terror passed, but soon it was followed by another wave. This wave was different. It flooded my soul with unspeakable peace, a peace that brought instant rest and repose to my troubled spirit. At once I was comfortable. I wanted to linger there. To say nothing. To do nothing. Simply to bask in the presence of God.

That moment was life transforming. Something deep in my spirit was being settled once for all. From this moment there could be no turning back; there could be no erasure of the indelible imprint of its power. I was alone with God. A holy God. An awesome God. A God who could fill me with terror in one second and with peace in the next. I knew in that hour that I had tasted of the Holy Grail. Within me was born a new thirst that could never be fully satisfied in this world. I resolved to learn more, to pursue this God who lived in dark Gothic cathedrals and who invaded my dormitory room to rouse me from complacent slumber.

What makes a college student seek the presence of God in the late hours? Something happened in a classroom that afternoon that drove me to the chapel. I was a new Christian. My conversion had been sudden and dramatic, a replica for me of the Damascus Road. My life had been turned upside down, and I was filled with zeal for the sweetness of Christ. I was consumed with a new passion. To study Scripture. To learn how to pray. To conquer the vices that assaulted my character. To grow in grace. I wanted desperately to make my life count for Christ. My soul was singing, "Lord, I want to be a Christian."

But something was missing in my early Christian life. I had abundant zeal, but it was marked by a shallowness, a kind of simplicity that was making me a one-dimensional person. I was a Unitarian of sorts, a Unitarian of the second person of the Trinity. I knew who Jesus was, but God the Father was shrouded in mystery. He was hidden, an enigma to my mind and a stranger to my soul. A dark veil covered His face.

My philosophy class changed that.

It was a course that had held little interest for me. I could hardly wait to get the tedious requirement behind me. I had chosen to major in Bible and thought the abstract speculations that went on in philosophy class were a waste of time. Listening to philosophers quarrel about reason and doubt seemed empty. I found no food for my soul, nothing to inflame my imagination, just dull and difficult intellectual puzzles that left me cold. Until that winter afternoon.

The lecture that day was about a Christian philosopher whose name was Aurelius Augustine. In the course of history, he had been canonized by the Roman Catholic church. Everyone spoke of him as Saint Augustine. The professor lectured on Augustine's views of the creation of the world.

I was familiar with the biblical account of creation. I knew that the Old Testament opens with the words, "In the beginning God created the heavens and the earth." But I had never thought deeply about the original act of creation. Augustine probed into this glorious mystery and raised the question, "How was it done?"

"In the beginning . . ."

It sounds like the start of a fairy tale: "Once upon a time." The trouble is that in the beginning there was no time as we understand it to be "once upon." We think of beginnings as starting points somewhere in the middle of a period of history. Cinderella had a mother and a grandmother. Her story that began "once upon a time" did not begin at the absolute beginning. Before Cinderella there were kings and queens, rocks and trees, horses, jackrabbits, daffodils.

What was there before the beginning of Genesis 1? The people God created had no parents or grandparents. They had no history books to read because there was no history. Before the creation there were no kings or queens or rocks or trees. There was nothing; nothing, of course, except God.

Here is where I got an Excedrin headache in my philosophy class. Before the world began, there was nothing. But what in the world is "nothing"? Have you ever tried to think about nothing? Where can we find it? Obviously nowhere. Why? Because it is nothing, and nothing doesn't exist. It can't exist, because if it did, then it would be something and not nothing. Are you starting to get a headache like mine? Think about it for a second. I can't tell you to think about "it" because nothing isn't an "it." I can only say "nothing isn't."

So how can we think about nothing? We can't. It is simply impossible. If we try to think of nothing, we always wind up thinking of something. As soon as I try to think about nothing, I start imagining a lot of "empty" air. But air is something. It has weight and substance. I know that because of what happens if a nail goes through the tire of my car.

Jonathan Edwards once said that nothing is what sleeping rocks dream about. That doesn't help much. My son offered me a better definition of *nothing*. When he was in junior high, I asked him when he came home from school, "What did you do today, Son?" The reply was the same every day: "Nuthin." So the best explanation I can give of "nothing" is "that which my son used to do every day in junior high."

Our understanding of creativity involves the shaping and forming of paint, clay, notes on paper, or some other substance. In our experience we have not been able to find a painter who paints without paint or a writer who writes without words or a composer who composes without notes. Artists must start with *something.* What artists do is shape, form, or rearrange other materials. But they never work with nothing.

Saint Augustine taught that God created the world out of nothing. Creation was something like the magician pulling a rabbit out of a hat. Except God didn't have a rabbit, and He didn't even have a hat.

My next-door neighbor is a skilled cabinetmaker. One of his specialties is constructing cabinets for professional magicians. He has given me a tour of his workshop and has shown me how the magician's boxes and cabinets are made. The trick is the clever use of mirrors. When the magician walks onstage and displays an empty box or an empty hat, what you see is only half the box or half the hat. Take the "empty" hat, for example. A mirror is fixed in the exact middle of the hat. The mirror reflects the empty side of the hat, giving an exact mirror image. The illusion creates the visual effect of seeing both sides of an empty hat. In fact you see only half the hat. The other half has plenty of room to conceal snow-white doves or a plump rabbit. Not much magic to it, is there?

God did not create the world with mirrors. To do that He would have required half a world to start with and a giant mirror to conceal the other half. Creation involved the bringing into existence of everything that is, including mirrors. God created the world from nothing. Once there was nothing, then suddenly, by the command of God, there was a universe.

Again we ask, How did He do it? The only hint the Bible gives is that God called the universe into being. Augustine called that act the "divine imperative" or the "divine fiat." We all know that an imperative is a command. So is a fiat. When Augustine spoke of a fiat, he was not thinking of a little Italian car. The dictionary defines *fiat* as a command or an act of the will that creates something.

At the present moment I am writing this book on a computer manufactured by IBM. It is an amazing piece of machinery, quite complicated in all its parts. The machine is designed to respond to certain commands. If I make a mistake while I am typing on the keyboard, I do not have to reach for an eraser. To correct my errors, I merely punch in a command, and the computer corrects it. The computer works by fiat. But the power of my fiat is limited. The only fiats that work are the ones that are already programmed into the computer. I would love simply to be able to say to the computer, "Write this whole book for me, please, while I go out and play golf." My machine can't do that. I can yell at the screen with the strongest imperative I know: "Write that book!" but the thing is too obstinate to comply.

God's fiats are not so limited. He can create by the sheer force of His divine command. He can bring something out of nothing, life out of death. He can do these things by the sound of His voice.

The first sound uttered in the universe was the voice of God commanding, "Let there be!" It is improper to say that this was the first sound "in" the universe because until the sound was made there was no universe for it to be in. God shouted into a void. Perhaps it was a kind of primal scream directed at the empty darkness.

The command created its own molecules to carry the sound waves of God's voice farther and farther into space. Yet sound waves would take too long. The speed of this imperative exceeded the speed of light. As soon as the words left the Creator's mouth, things began to happen. Where His voice reverberated, stars appeared, glowing in unspeakable brilliance in tempo with the songs of angels. The force of divine energy splattered against the sky like a kaleidoscope of color hurled from the palette of a powerful artist. Comets crisscrossed the sky with flashing tails like Fourth of July skyrockets.

The act of creation was the first event in history. It was also the most dazzling. The Supreme Architect gazed at His complex blueprint and shouted commands for the boundaries of the world to be set. He spoke, and the seas were shut behind doors, and the clouds were filled with dew. He bound the Pleiades and buckled the belt of Orion. He spoke again, and the earth began to fill with orchards in full bloom. Blossoms burst forth like springtime in Mississippi. The lavender hues of plum trees danced with the brilliance of azaleas and forsythia.

God spoke once more, and the waters teemed with living things. The snail sneaked beneath the shadowy form of the stingray, while the great marlin broke the surface of the water to promenade on the waves with his tail. Again He spoke, and the roar of the lion and the bleating of sheep were heard. Four-footed animals, eight-legged spiders, and winged insects appeared.

And God said, "That's good."

Then God stooped to earth and carefully fashioned a piece of clay. He lifted it gently to His lips and breathed into it. The clay began to move. It began to think. It began to feel. It began to worship. It was alive and stamped with the image of its Creator.

Consider the raising of Lazarus from the dead. How did Jesus do it? He did not enter the tomb where the rotting corpse of Lazarus was laid out; He did not have to administer mouth-to-mouth resuscitation. He stood outside the tomb, at a distance, and cried with a loud voice, "Lazarus, come forth!" Blood began to flow through the veins of Lazarus, and brain waves started to pulsate. In a burst of life Lazarus quit his grave and walked out. That is fiat creation, the power of the divine imperative.

Some modern theorists believe that the world was created by nothing. Note the difference between saying that the world was created *from* nothing and saying that the universe was created *by* nothing. In this modern view the rabbit comes out of the hat without a rabbit, a hat, or even a magician. The modern view is far more miraculous than the biblical view. It suggests that nothing created something. More than that, it holds that nothing created everything—quite a feat indeed!

Now surely there aren't serious people running around in this scientific age claiming that the universe was created by nothing, are there? Yes. Scores of them.

To be sure, they usually don't say it quite the way I have said it, and they'd probably be annoyed with me for stating their views in such a manner. They'd undoubtedly protest that I have given a distorted caricature of their sophisticated position. Okay. True—they don't say that the universe was created by nothing; they say that the universe was created by chance.

But chance is no thing. It has no weight, no measurements, no power. It is merely a word we use to describe mathematical possibilities. It can do nothing. It can do nothing because it is nothing. To say that the universe was created by chance is to say that it came from nothing.

That is intellectual madness. What are the chances that the universe was created by chance?

Saint Augustine understood that the world could not be created by chance. He knew that it required something or someone with power—the very power of creation—to get the job done. He knew that something cannot come from nothing. He understood that somewhere, somehow, something or someone had to have the power of being. If not, then nothing would now exist.

The Bible says, "In the beginning God." The God we worship is the God who has always been. He alone can create beings, because He alone has the *power of being.* He is not nothing. He is not chance. He is pure Being, the One who has the power to be *all by Himself.* He alone is eternal. He alone has power over death. He alone can call worlds into being by fiat, by the power of His command. Such power is staggering, awesome. It is deserving of respect, of humble adoration.

It was the words of Augustine—that God created the world out of nothing by the sheer power of His voice—that drove me to the chapel at midnight.

I know what it means to be converted. I know what it means to be born again. I also understand that a person can be born again only once. When the Holy Spirit quickens our souls to new life in Christ, He does not stop His work. He continues to work on us. He continues to change us.

My experience in the classroom, thinking about the creation of the world, was like being born again a second time. It was like being converted, not merely to God the Son, but to God the Father. Suddenly I had a passion to know God the Father. I wanted to know Him in His majesty, to know Him in His power, to know Him in His august holiness.

My "conversion" to God the Father was not without its attending difficulties. Though I was deeply impressed by the notion of a God who created a whole universe from nothing, I was troubled by the fact that the world we live in is a place filled with sorrows. It is a world riddled with evil. My next question was, How could a good and holy God create a world that is in such a mess? As I studied the Old Testament, I was also bothered by the stories about God's ordering the slaughter of women and children, of God's killing Uzzah instantly for touching the ark of the covenant, and by other narratives that seemed to reveal a brutal side to the character of God. How could I ever come to love such a God?

The one concept, the central idea I kept meeting

in Scripture, was the idea that God is *holy*. The word was foreign to me. I wasn't sure what it meant. I made the question a matter of diligent and persistent search. Today I am still absorbed with the question of the holiness of God. I am convinced that it is one of the most important ideas that a Christian can ever grapple with. It is basic to our whole understanding of God and of Christianity.

The idea of holiness is so central to biblical teaching that it is said of God, "Holy is his name" (Luke 1:49). His name is holy because He is holy. He is not always treated with holy reverence. His name is tramped through the dirt of this world. It functions as a curse word, a platform for the obscene. That the world has little respect for God is vividly seen by the way the world regards His name. No honor. No reverence. No awe before Him.

If I were to ask a group of Christians what the top priority of the church is, I am sure I would get a wide variety of answers. Some would say evangelism, others social action, and still others spiritual nurture. But I have yet to hear anyone talk about what Jesus' priorities were.

What is the first petition of the Lord's Prayer? Jesus said, "This, then, is how you should pray: 'Our Father in heaven . . .'" (Matt. 6:9). The first line of the prayer is not a petition. It is a form of personal address. The prayer continues: "hallowed be your name, your kingdom come" (Matt. 6:9-10). We often confuse the words "hallowed be your name" with part of the address, as if the words were "hallowed *is* your name." In that case the words would merely be an ascription of praise to God. But that is not how Jesus said it. He uttered it as a petition, as the first petition. We should be praying that God's name be hallowed, that God be regarded as holy.

There is a kind of sequence within the prayer. God's kingdom will never come where His name is not considered holy. His will is not done on earth as it is in heaven if His name is desecrated here. In heaven the name of God is holy. It is breathed by angels in a sacred hush. Heaven is a place where reverence for God is total. It is foolish to look for the kingdom anywhere God is not revered.

How we understand the person and character of God the Father affects every aspect of our lives. It affects far more than what we normally call the "religious" aspects of our lives. If God is the Creator of the entire universe, then it must follow that He is the Lord of the whole universe. No part of the world is outside of His lordship. That means that no part of my life must be outside of His lordship. His holy character has something to say about economics, politics, athletics, romance—everything with which we are involved.

God is inescapable. There is no place we can hide from Him. Not only does He penetrate every aspect of our lives, but He penetrates it in His majestic holiness. Therefore we must seek to understand what the holy is. We dare not seek to avoid it. There can be no worship, no spiritual growth, no true obedience without it. It defines our goal as Christians. God has declared, "Be holy, because I am holy" (Lev. 11:44).

To reach that goal, we must understand what holiness is.

Allowing God's Holiness to Touch Our Lives

As you reflect about what you have learned and redis-covered about God's holiness, answer these questions. Use a journal to record your responses to God's holi-ness, or discuss your responses with a friend.

1. When you think of God as holy, what comes to your mind?
2. Describe a time when you were overcome by God's holiness.
3. Are you attracted to God's holiness?
4. What does it mean for you to be holy in the coming week?

CHAPTER TWO

Holy, Holy, Holy

Weave a circle round him thrice,

And close your eyes with holy dread.

For he on honey-dew hath fed,

And drunk the milk of Paradise.

SAMUEL TAYLOR COLERIDGE

The prophet in Old Testament Israel was a lonely man. He was a rugged individualist singled out by God for a painful task. He served as a prosecuting attorney of sorts, the appointed spokesman of the Supreme Judge of heaven and earth to bring suit against those who had sinned against the bench.

The prophet was not an earthly philosopher who wrote his opinions for scholars to discuss; he was not a playwright who composed dramas for public entertainment. He was a messenger, a herald of a cosmic king. His announcements were prefaced by the words "Thus says the Lord" (NASB).

The record of the lives of the prophets reads like a history of martyrs. Their history sounds like a casualty report from the Third Division in World War II. The life expectancy of a prophet was that of a marine lieutenant in combat.

When it is said of Jesus that "He was despised and rejected by men, a man of sorrows, and familiar with suffering" (Isa. 53:3), it is clear that He stood in a long line of men whom God had appointed to such suffering. The prophet's curse was solitude; his home was often a cave. The desert was his traditional meeting place with God. Nakedness was sometimes his wardrobe, a wooden stock his necktie. His songs were composed with tears.

Such a man was Isaiah ben Amoz.

In the panoply of Old Testament heroes, Isaiah stands out in stellar relief. He was a prophet of prophets, a leader of leaders. He is called a "major prophet" because of the vast size of the written material that bears his name.

As a prophet, Isaiah was unusual. Most prophets were of humble origins: peasants, shepherds, farmers. Isaiah was of the nobility. He was a recognized statesman, having access to the royal court of his day. He consorted with princes and kings. God used him to speak to several monarchs of Judah, including Uzziah, Jotham, Ahaz, and Hezekiah.

What set a prophet of Israel apart from all other men was the sacred auspices of his call. His call was not from men. He could not apply for the job. He had to be selected—chosen directly and immediately by God. And the call was sovereign; it could not be refused. (Jeremiah tried to refuse his call but was abruptly reminded by God that He had consecrated Jeremiah from his mother's womb. When, after a term in this office, Jeremiah sought to resign, God refused to accept his resignation.) The job of prophet was for life. There was no quitting or retiring with pension.

The record of the call of Isaiah is perhaps the most dramatic of all such calls recorded for us in the Old Testament. We are told that it came to pass in the year that King Uzziah died.

King Uzziah died in the eighth century B.C. His

reign was important in Jewish history. He was one of the better kings who ruled over Judah. He was not a David, but neither was he noted for the corruption that characterized the kings of the north, such as Ahab. Uzziah ascended to the throne when he was sixteen years old. He reigned in Jerusalem for fifty-two years. Think of it, fifty-two years! In the past fifty-two years, the United States has witnessed the administrations of Truman, Eisenhower, Kennedy, Johnson, Nixon, Ford, Carter, Reagan, Bush, Clinton, and Bush. But many people in Jerusalem lived their entire lives under the reign of King Uzziah.

The Bible tells us that Uzziah began his reign in godliness, doing "what was right in the eyes of the LORD" (2 Chron. 26:4). He sought after God, and God blessed him. He was victorious in battle over the Philistines and other nations. He built towers in Jerusalem and strengthened the city walls. He dug massive cisterns in the desert and stimulated great expansion in the nation's agriculture. He restored the military power of Judah to a standard almost as high as it had been under David. For most of his career Uzziah was noted as a great and beloved king.

The story of Uzziah ends with a sad note, however. The last years of his life were like those of a Shakespearean tragic hero. His career was marred by the sin of pride committed after he acquired great wealth and power. He tried to play God. He boldly entered the temple and arrogantly claimed for himself the rights that God had given only to the priests. When the priests of the temple tried to stop his act of sacrilege, Uzziah became enraged. While he was screaming at them in fury, leprosy broke out on his forehead. The Bible says of him: "He lived in a separate house, being a leper,... cut off from the house of the LORD" (2 Chron. 26:21, NASB). When Uzziah died, in spite of the shame of his later years, it was a time of national mourning. Isaiah went to the temple, presumably looking for consolation in a time of national and personal grief. He got more than he bargained for: "In the year that King Uzziah died, I saw the Lord seated on a throne, high and exalted, and the train of his robe filled the temple" (Isa. 6:1).

The king was dead. But when Isaiah entered the temple, he saw another king, the Ultimate King, the One who sat forever on the throne of Judah. He saw the Lord.

Notice how in Isaiah 6:1 the word *Lord* is printed. It begins with a capital letter and then is finished with lowercase letters. This stands in contrast with the word LORD that occurs later in the text and frequently in Scripture. Sometimes the word *Lord* appears in all capital letters—LORD. This is not an error in printing or a mere inconsistency on the part of the translator. Most English translations of the Bible follow this device of rendering the word *Lord* sometimes in lowercase letters and other times in uppercase letters. The reason for this difference is that two different Hebrew words are used in the original text, but both are rendered in English by the word *Lord*.

When the word *Lord* occurs in lowercase letters, the translator is indicating to us that the word *adonai* is found in the Hebrew Bible. Adonai means "sovereign one." It is not the name of God. It is a title for God, indeed the supreme title given to God in the Old Testament. When LORD appears in all capital letters it indicates that the word *Jahweh* is used in the Old Testament. Jahweh is the sacred name of God, the name by which God revealed Himself to Moses in the burning bush. This is the unspeakable name, the ineffable name, the holy name that is guarded from profanity in the life of Israel. Normally it occurs only with the use of its four consonants—*yhwh*. It is therefore referred to as the sacred tetragrammaton, the unspeakable four letters.

We see, for example, this contrast in words found in the Psalms. Psalm 8 reads, "O LORD, our Lord, how majestic is your name in all the earth!" (Ps. 8:1). What the Jew was saying was, "O Jahweh, our Adonai, how excellent is your name in all the earth." Or we could render it, "O God, our sovereign one, how excellent. . . ." Again we read in Psalm 110: "The LORD says to my Lord: 'Sit at my right hand' " (Ps. 110:1). Here the psalmist is saying, "God said to my sovereign, sit at my right hand."

LORD is the name of God; *Lord* is His title. We speak of President George W. Bush. *George* is his name; *president* is his title. If the highest office in our land is the office of president, so the highest office and title in Israel was the office of Sovereign. The title *adonai* was reserved for God. It was the title that was given to Jesus in the New Testament. When Christ is called "Lord," He is invested with the New Testament equivalent of the Old Testament *adonai*. Jesus is called the King of kings and Lord of lords, gaining a title that beforehand was reserved only for God the Father, the supreme Sovereign of heaven and earth.

These different uses of the words LORD and Lord indicate the care with which people communicated God's holy nature. In some ways that is similar to my choosing to use capital letters when I use a pronoun to refer to God. Because God is unspeakably holy, I cannot bring myself to refer to Him as "him," even though my younger readers may be bothered by what they perceive to be an outdated use of capital letters. To me it is a gesture of respect and awe for a holy God.

When Isaiah came to the temple, there was a crisis of sovereignty in the land. Uzziah was dead. The eyes of Isaiah were opened to see the real king of the nation. He saw God seated on the throne, the sovereign one.

Humans are not allowed to see the face of God. The Scriptures warn that no person can see God and live. We remember Moses' request when he ascended the holy mountain of God. Moses had been an eyewitness of astonishing miracles. He had heard the voice of God speaking to him out of the burning bush. He had witnessed the river Nile turn into blood. He had tasted manna from heaven and had gazed upon the pillar of cloud and the pillar of fire. He had seen the chariots of Pharaoh inundated by the waves of the Red Sea. Still he was not satisfied. He wanted more. He craved the ultimate spiritual experience. He inquired of the Lord on the mountain, "Let me see your face. Show me your glory." The request was denied:

And the LORD said, "I will cause all my
goodness to pass in front of you, and I
will proclaim my name, the LORD, in your
presence. I will have mercy on whom I will
have mercy, and I will have compassion on
whom I will have compassion. But," he said,
"you cannot see my face, for no one may see
me and live." Then the LORD said, "There is a
place near me where you may stand on a rock.
When my glory passes by, I will put you in a
cleft in the rock and cover you with my hand
until I have passed by. Then I will remove my
hand and you will see my back; but my face
must not be seen." (Exod. 33:19-23)

When God told Moses that he could see His back,
the literal reading of the text can be translated "hind-
quarters." God allowed Moses to see His hindquar-
ters but never His face. When Moses returned from
the mount, his face was shining. The people were
terrified, and they shrank away from him in horror.
Moses' face was too dazzling for them to look upon.
So Moses put a veil over his face so that the people
could approach him. This experience of terror was
directed at the face of a man who had come so close
to God that he was reflecting God's glory. This was a
reflection of the glory from the back of God, not the
refulgent glory of His face. If people are terrified by
the sight of the reflected glory of the back parts of
God, how can anyone stand to gaze directly into His
holy face?

Yet the final goal of every Christian is to be allowed

to see what was denied to Moses. We want to see Him face-to-face. We want to bask in the radiant glory of His divine countenance. It was the hope of every Jew, a hope instilled in the most famous and beloved benediction of Israel: "The LORD bless you and keep you; the LORD make his face shine upon you and be gracious to you; the LORD turn his face toward you and give you peace" (Num. 6:24-26).

This hope, crystallized in the benediction of Israel, becomes more than a hope for the Christian—it becomes a promise. John tells in his first letter: "We are children of God, and what we will be has not yet been made known. But we know that when he appears, we shall be like him, for we shall see him as he is" (1 John 3:2). Here is the promise of God: We shall see Him as He is. Theologians call this future expectation the beatific vision. We will see God *as He is.* This means that someday we will see God face-to-face. We will not see the reflected glory of a burning bush or a pillar of cloud. We will see Him as He is, as He is in His pure, divine essence.

Right now it is impossible for us to see God in His pure essence. Before that can ever happen, we must be purified. When Jesus taught the Beatitudes, He promised only a distinct group the vision of God: "Blessed are the pure in heart, for they will see God" (Matt. 5:8). None of us in this world is pure in heart. It is our impurity that prevents us from seeing God. The problem is not with our eyes; it is with our hearts. Only after we are purified and totally sanctified in heaven will we have the capacity to gaze upon Him face-to-face.

> Above him were seraphs, each with six wings:
> With two wings they covered their faces, with
> two they covered their feet, and with two they
> were flying. (Isa. 6:2)

The seraphim are not sinful humans burdened with impure hearts. Yet as angelic beings, they are still creatures, and even in their lofty status as consorts of the heavenly host it is necessary for them to shield their eyes from a direct gaze on the face of God. They are fearfully and wonderfully made, equipped by their Creator with a special pair of wings to cover their faces in His majestic presence.

The seraphim have a second pair of wings. The second pair is used to cover their feet. This equipment is not intended as a sort of angelic shoe to protect the soles of their feet or to facilitate walking in the heavenly temple. The covering of the feet is for a different reason, a reason reminiscent of Moses' experience with the burning bush:

> There the angel of the LORD appeared to him
> in flames of fire from within a bush. Moses
> saw that though the bush was on fire it did not
> burn up. So Moses thought, "I will go over and
> see this strange sight—why the bush does not
> burn up."
>
> When the LORD saw that he had gone over to
> look, God called to him from within the bush,
> "Moses, Moses!"
>
> And Moses said, "Here I am."

> "Do not come any closer," God said. "Take
> off your sandals, for the place where you are
> standing is holy ground." (Exod. 3:2-5)

God commanded Moses to take off his shoes.
Moses was standing on holy ground. The ground was
made holy by the presence of God. The act of remov-
ing the shoes was a symbol of Moses' recognition that
he was of the earth—earthy. Human feet, sometimes
called "feet of clay," symbolize our creatureliness. It is
our feet that link us to the earth.

The seraphim are not of the earth. Their feet are
not made of clay. As angels, they are spirit beings.
Nevertheless they remain creatures, and the imagery
of Isaiah's vision suggests that they too must cover
their feet, acknowledging their creatureliness in the
exalted presence of God.

Here we encounter the crux of Isaiah's vision. It is
the song of the seraphim that reveals the awesome
message of this text. "And they were calling to one
another: 'Holy, holy, holy is the LORD Almighty; the
whole earth is full of his glory' " (Isa. 6:3). The song
is the repetition of a single word—*holy.* Three times
the word is sung in succession, giving the church its
most august anthem. The song is called the *Trisagion,*
which means simply the "three times holy."

The significance of the repetition of the word *holy*
can be easily missed. It represents a peculiar literary
device that is found in Hebrew forms of literature,
especially in poetry. The repetition is a form of emphasis. When we want to emphasize the importance
of something in English, we have several devices from

which to choose. We may underline the important words or print them in italics or boldface type. We may attach an exclamation point following the words or set them off in quotation marks. These are all devices to call the reader's attention to something that is especially important.

The Old Testament Jew also had different techniques to indicate emphasis. One such device was the method of repetition. We see Jesus' use of repetition with the words "Truly, truly, I say to you" (NASB). Here the double use of *truly* was a sign that what He was about to say was of crucial importance. The word translated "truly" is the ancient word *amen*. We normally think of the word *amen* as something people say at the end of a sermon or of a prayer. It means simply, "It is true." Jesus used it as a preface instead of a response.

A humorous use of the repetition device may be seen in Genesis 14. The story of the battle of the kings in the Valley of Siddim mentions men who fell in the great tar pits of the region. Some translators call them asphalt pits, or bitumen pits, or simply great pits. Why the confusion in translation? Exactly what kind of pits were they? The Hebrew is unclear. The original text gives the Hebrew word for pit and then simply repeats it. The story speaks literally of pit pits. The Jew was saying that there are pits and there are pits. Some pits are pittier than other pits. These pits—the pit pits—were the pittiest pits of all. It is one thing to fall into a pit. But if you fall into a pit pit, you are in deep trouble.

On a handful of occasions the Bible repeats something to the third degree. To mention something three times in succession is to elevate it to the superlative degree, to attach to it emphasis of superimportance. For example, the dreadful judgment of God is declared in the book of Revelation by the eagle who cried in midair with a loud voice: "Woe! Woe! Woe to the inhabitants of the earth" (Rev. 8:13). Or we hear it in the mocking sarcasm of Jeremiah's temple speech when he chided the people for calling out in hypocrisy, "This is the temple of the LORD, the temple of the LORD, the temple of the LORD!" (Jer. 7:4).

Only once in sacred Scripture is an attribute of God elevated to the third degree. Only once is a characteristic of God mentioned three times in succession. The Bible says that God is holy, holy, holy. Not that He is merely holy, or even holy, holy. He is holy, holy, holy. The Bible never says that God is love, love, love; or mercy, mercy, mercy; or wrath, wrath, wrath; or justice, justice, justice. It does say that He is holy, holy, holy, that the whole earth is full of His glory.

> At the sound of their voices the doorposts and thresholds shook and the temple was filled with smoke. (Isa. 6:4)

A recent survey of people who used to be church members revealed that the main reason they stopped going to church was that they found it boring. It is difficult for many people to find worship a thrilling and moving experience. We note here, when God appeared in the temple, the doors and the thresholds were moved. The inert matter of doorposts, the inanimate thresholds, the wood and metal that could neither hear nor speak had the good sense to be moved by the presence of God. The literal meaning of the text is that they were shaken. They began to quake where they stood.

> "Woe to me!" I cried. "I am ruined! For I am a man of unclean lips, and I live among a people of unclean lips, and my eyes have seen the King, the LORD Almighty." (Isa. 6:5)

The doors of the temple were not the only things that were shaking. The thing that quaked the most in the building was the body of Isaiah. When he saw the living God, the reigning monarch of the universe displayed before his eyes in all of His holiness, Isaiah cried out, "Woe is me!"

The cry of Isaiah sounds strange to the modern ear. It is rare that we hear people today use the word *woe.* Since this word is old-fashioned and archaic, some modern translators have preferred to substitute another word in its place. That is a serious mistake. The word *woe* is a crucial biblical word that we cannot afford to ignore. It has a special meaning.

When we think of woes, we think of the troubles encountered in melodramas set in the old-time nickelodeons. *The Perils of Pauline* showed the heroine wringing her hands in anguish as the heartless landlord came to foreclose on her mortgage. Or we think of Mighty Mouse flying from his cloud to streak to the rescue of his girlfriend, who is being tied to the railroad tracks by Oilcan Harry. She cries, "Woe is me!"

The term *woe* has gone the way of other worn-out exclamations like *alas* or *alack* or *forsooth*. The only language that has kept the expression in current usage is Yiddish. Modern Jews still declare their frustrations by exclaiming "Oy vay!" which is a shortened version of the full expression *oy vay ist mer*. Oy vay is Yiddish for "Oh woe," an abbreviation for the full expression, "Oh woe is me!"

The full force of Isaiah's exclamation must be seen against the background of a special form of speech found in the Bible. When prophets announced their messages, the most frequent form the divine utterances took was the *oracle*. The oracles were announcements from God; they could be good news or bad news. The positive oracles were prefaced by the word *blessed*. When Jesus preached the Sermon on the Mount, He used the form of the oracle, saying, "Blessed are the poor in spirit," "Blessed are those who mourn," "Blessed are those who hunger and thirst." His audience understood that He was using the formula of the prophet, the oracle that brought good tidings.

Jesus also used the negative form of the oracle. When He spoke out in angry denunciation of the Pharisees, He pronounced the judgment of God upon their heads by saying to them, "Woe to you, scribes and Pharisees, hypocrites!" (Matt. 23:13-29, NASB). He said this so often that it began to sound like a litany. On the lips of a prophet the word *woe* is an announcement of doom. In the Bible, cities are doomed, nations are doomed, individuals are doomed—all by uttering the oracle of woe.

Isaiah's use of *woe* was extraordinary. When he saw the Lord, he pronounced the judgment of God upon himself. "Woe to me!" he cried, calling down the curse of God, the utter anathema of judgment and doom upon his own head. It was one thing for a prophet to curse another person in the name of God; it was quite another for a prophet to put that curse upon himself.

Immediately following the curse of doom, Isaiah cried, "I am ruined." I prefer the older translation that read, "For I am undone." We can readily see why more modern translations have made the change from *undone* to *ruined*. Nobody speaks today about being undone. But the word is more vivid in what it conveys than the word *ruined*.

To be undone means to come apart at the seams, to be unraveled. What Isaiah was expressing is what modern psychologists describe as the experience of personal disintegration. To disintegrate means exactly what the word suggests, *dis integrate*. To integrate something is to put pieces together into a unified whole. When schools are integrated, children from two different races are placed together to form one student body. The word *integrity* comes from this root, suggesting a person whose life is whole or wholesome. In modern slang we say, "That person has got it all together."

If ever there was a man of integrity, it was Isaiah ben Amoz. He was a whole man, a together type of a fellow. He was considered by his contemporaries as the most righteous man in the nation. He was respected as a paragon of virtue. Then he caught one sudden glimpse of a holy God. In that single moment, all of his self-esteem was shattered. In a brief second he was exposed, made naked beneath the gaze of the absolute standard of holiness. As long as Isaiah could compare himself to other mortals, he was able to sustain a lofty opinion of his own character. The instant he measured himself by the ultimate standard, he was destroyed— morally and spiritually annihilated. He was undone. He came apart. His sense of integrity collapsed.

The sudden realization of ruin was linked to Isaiah's mouth. He cried, "I am a man of unclean lips." Strange. We might have expected him to say, "I am a man of unclean habits," or, "I am a man of unclean thoughts." Instead he called attention immediately to his mouth. In effect he said, "I have a dirty mouth." Why this focus on his mouth?

Perhaps a clue to Isaiah's utterance may be found in the words of Jesus when He said that it's not what goes into people's mouths that defiles them; it's what comes out of their mouths that defiles them. Or we could look to the discourse on the tongue written by James, the Lord's brother:

> The tongue also is a fire, a world of evil among the parts of the body. It corrupts the whole person, sets the whole course of his life on fire, and is itself set on fire by hell. All kinds of animals, birds, reptiles and creatures of the sea are being tamed and have been tamed by man, but no man can tame the tongue. It is a restless evil, full of deadly poison. With the tongue we praise our Lord and Father, and

with it we curse men, who have been made in God's likeness. Out of the same mouth come praise and cursing. My brothers, this should not be. Can both fresh water and salt water flow from the same spring? My brothers, can a fig tree bear olives, or a grapevine bear figs? Neither can a salt spring produce fresh water. (James 3:6-12)

The tongue is a restless evil, full of deadly poison. This was the realization of Isaiah. He recognized that he was not alone in his dilemma. He understood that the whole nation was infected with dirty mouths: "I live among a people of unclean lips." In the flash of the moment Isaiah had a new and radical understanding of sin. He saw that it was pervasive, in himself and in everyone else.

We are fortunate in one respect: God does not appear to us in the way He appeared to Isaiah. Who could stand it? God normally reveals our sinfulness to us a bit at a time. We experience a gradual recognition of our own corruption. God showed Isaiah his corruption all at once. No wonder he was ruined.

Isaiah explained it this way: "My eyes have seen the King, the LORD Almighty" (Isa. 6:5). He saw the holiness of God. For the first time in his life Isaiah really understood who God was. At the same instant, for the first time Isaiah really understood who Isaiah was.

Then one of the seraphs flew to me with a live coal in his hand, which he had taken with

tongs from the altar. With it he touched my
mouth and said, "See, this has touched your
lips; your guilt is taken away and your sin
atoned for." (Isa. 6:6-7)

Isaiah was groveling on the floor. Every nerve fiber
in his body was trembling. He was looking for a place
to hide, praying that somehow the earth would cover
him or the roof of the temple would fall upon him—
anything to get him out from under the holy gaze of
God. But there was nowhere to hide. He was naked
and alone before God. Unlike Adam, Isaiah had no
Eve to comfort him, no fig leaves to conceal him. His
was pure moral anguish, the kind that rips out the
heart of a man and tears his soul to pieces. Guilt, guilt,
guilt. Relentless guilt screamed from his every pore.

The holy God is also a God of grace. He refused
to allow His servant to continue on his belly without comfort. He took immediate steps to cleanse the
man and restore his soul. He commanded one of the
seraphim to jump into action. The angelic creature
moved swiftly, flying to the altar with tongs. From the
burning fire, the seraph took a glowing coal, too hot
to touch even for an angel, and flew to Isaiah.

The seraph pressed the white-hot coal to the lips
of the prophet and seared them. The lips are one of
the most sensitive parts of human flesh, the meeting point of the kiss. Here Isaiah felt the holy flame
burning his mouth. The acrid smell of burning flesh
filled his nostrils, but that sensation was dulled by the
excruciating pain of the heat. This was a severe mercy,
a painful act of cleansing. Isaiah's wound was being

cauterized, the dirt in his mouth was being burned away. He was refined by holy fire.

In this divine act of cleansing, Isaiah experienced a forgiveness that went beyond the purification of his lips. He was cleansed throughout, forgiven to the core, but not without the awful pain of repentance. He went beyond cheap grace and the easy utterance "I'm sorry." He was in mourning for his sin, overcome with moral grief, and God sent an angel to heal him. His sin was taken away. His dignity remained intact. His guilt was removed, but his humanity was not insulted. The conviction that he felt was constructive. His was no cruel and unusual punishment. A second of burning flesh on the lips brought a healing that would extend to eternity. In a moment, the disintegrated prophet was whole again. His mouth was purged. He was clean.

> Then I heard the voice of the Lord saying,
> "Whom shall I send? And who will go for us?"
> And I said, "Here am I. Send me!" (Isa. 6:8)

Isaiah's vision took on a new dimension. Until this point he had seen the glory of God; he had heard the song of the seraphim; he had felt the burning coal upon his lips. Now for the first time he heard the voice of God. Suddenly the angels were silent, and the voice boomed throughout the temple, the voice that Scripture elsewhere describes as the sound of many waters. That voice echoed with the piercing questions: "Whom shall I send? And who will go for us?"

There is a pattern here, a pattern repeated in history.

God appears, people quake in terror, God forgives and heals, God sends. From brokenness to mission is the human pattern. When God asked, "Whom shall I *send*?" Isaiah understood the force of the word. To be "sent" meant to function as an emissary for God, to be a spokesman for the deity. In the New Testament the word *apostle* meant "one who is sent." The Old Testament counterpart to the New Testament apostle was the prophet. God was looking for a volunteer to enter the lonely, grueling office of prophet. "Whom shall I send?"

Notice Isaiah's answer: "Here am I, send me." There is a crucial difference between saying, "Here am I" and saying, "Here I am." Had he said, "Here I am," that would have merely indicated his location. But he was interested in more than giving God his location. He said, "Here am I." With these words Isaiah was stepping forward to volunteer. His answer was simply, "I will go. Look no further. Send me."

Two important things must be noted in Isaiah's reply. The first is that he was not Humpty-Dumpty. In the nursery rhyme the fall of Mr. Dumpty is tragic because no one in the entire kingdom had the power to put him together again. Yet he was no more fragile than Isaiah. Isaiah was shattered into as many pieces as any fallen egg. But God put him together again. God was able to take a shattered man and send him into the ministry. He took a sinful man and made him a prophet. He took a man with a dirty mouth and made him God's spokesman.

The second important thing we learn from this event is that God's work of grace on Isaiah's soul did not annihilate his personal identity. Isaiah said, "Here am I." Isaiah could still speak in terms of "I." He still had an identity. He still had a personality. Far from God seeking to destroy the "self," as many distortions of Christianity would claim, God redeems the self. He heals the self so that it may be useful and fulfilled in the mission to which the person is called. Isaiah's personality was overhauled but not annihilated. He was still Isaiah ben Amoz when he left the temple. He was the same person, but his mouth was clean.

Ministers are noteworthy of their calling. All preachers are vulnerable to the charge of hypocrisy. In fact, the more faithful preachers are to the Word of God in their preaching, the more liable they are to the charge of hypocrisy. Why? Because the more faithful people are to the Word of God, the higher the message is that they will preach. The higher the message, the further they will be from obeying it themselves.

I cringe inside when I speak in churches about the holiness of God. I can anticipate the responses of the people. They leave the sanctuary convinced that they have just been in the presence of a holy man. Because they hear me preach about holiness, they assume I must be as holy as the message I preach. That's when I want to cry, "Woe is me."

It's dangerous to assume that because a person is drawn to holiness in his study that he is thereby a holy man. There is irony here. I am sure that the reason I have a deep hunger to learn of the holiness of God is precisely because I am not holy. I am a profane man—a man who spends more time out of the temple than in it. But I have had just enough of a taste of the majesty of God to want more. I know what it means to be a forgiven man and what it means to be sent on a mission. My soul cries for more. My soul needs more.

Allowing God's Holiness to Touch Our Lives

As you reflect about what you have learned and rediscovered about God's holiness, answer these questions. Use a journal to record your responses to God's holiness, or discuss your responses with a friend.

1. Have you ever had an experience in which you were overcome by God's presence, in which you were "undone" by God's presence?
2. Isaiah's response to God's revelation of His holiness was, "Woe is me." What is your response?
3. In what ways do you need to be refined by the fire of God's holiness?
4. What aspect of God's holiness, as described in this chapter, causes you to worship Him more fully?
5. Use the hymn at the end of this book to express your worship to God.

CHAPTER THREE

The Fearful Mystery

What is that which gleams through me
and smites my heart without wounding it?
I am both a-shudder and aglow.
A-shudder, in so far as I am unlike it,
aglow in so far as I am like it.

St. Augustine

Here we are, already in the third chapter of this book, and I still have not defined what it means to be holy.

I wish I could postpone the task even further. The difficulties involved in defining holiness are vast. There is so much to holiness, and it is so foreign to us that the task seems almost impossible. In a very real sense, the word *holy* is a foreign word. But even when we run up against foreign words, we hope that a foreign language dictionary can rescue us by providing a clear translation. The problem we face, however, is that the word *holy* is foreign to all languages. No dictionary is adequate to the task.

Our problem with definition is made more difficult by the fact that in the Bible the word *holy* is used in more than one way. In a sense the Bible uses *holy* in a way that is very closely related to God's goodness. It has been customary to define *holy* as "purity, free from every stain, wholly perfect and immaculate in every detail."

Purity is the first word most of us think of when we hear the word *holy*. To be sure, the Bible does use the word this way. But the idea of purity or of moral perfection is at best the secondary meaning of the term in the Bible. When the seraphim sang their song, they were saying far more than that God was "purity, purity, purity."

The primary meaning of *holy* is "separate." It comes from an ancient word that means "to cut," or "to separate." To translate this basic meaning into contemporary language would be to use the phrase "a cut apart." Perhaps even more accurate would be the phrase "a cut above something." When we find a garment or another piece of merchandise that is outstanding, that has a superior excellence, we use the expression that it is "a cut above the rest."

God's holiness is more than just separateness. His holiness is also transcendent. The word *transcendence* means literally "to climb across." It is defined as "exceeding usual limits." To transcend is to rise above something, to go above and beyond a certain limit. When we speak of the transcendence of God, we are talking about that sense in which God is above and beyond us. Transcendence describes His supreme and absolute greatness. The word is used to describe God's relationship to the world. He is higher than the world. He has absolute power over the world. The world has no power over Him. Transcendence describes God in His consuming majesty, His exalted loftiness. It points to the infinite distance that separates Him from every creature. He is an infinite cut above everything else.

When the Bible calls God holy, it means primarily that God is transcendentally separate. He is so far above and beyond us that He seems almost totally foreign to us. To be holy is to be "other," to be different in a special way. The same basic meaning is used when the word *holy* is applied to earthly things. Look carefully at the following list of things the Bible speaks of as holy:

holy ground	holy nation
holy Sabbath	holy anointing oil
Holy Place	holy jubilee
holy linen coat	holy field
holy house	holy water
holy tithe	holy ark
holy censers	Holy City
holy bread	holy word
holy seed	holy ones
holy covenant	Holy of Holies
holy convocation	

This list is by no means exhaustive. It serves to show us that the word *holy* is applied to all sorts of things besides God. In every case the word *holy* is used to express something other than a moral or ethical quality. The things that are holy are things that are set apart, separated from the rest. They have been separated from the commonplace, consecrated to the Lord and to His service.

The things in the list are not holy in themselves. To become holy they first must be consecrated or sanctified by God. God alone is holy in Himself. Only God can sanctify something else. Only God can give the touch that changes it from the commonplace to something special, different, and apart.

Notice how the Old Testament regards things that have been made holy. Whatever is holy carries a peculiar character. It has been separated from a common use. It may not be touched; it may not be eaten; it may not be used for common matters. It is special.

Where does purity come in? We are so accustomed to equating holiness with purity or ethical perfection that we look for the idea when the word *holy* appears. When things are made holy, when they are consecrated, they are set apart unto purity. They are to be used in a pure way. They are to reflect purity as well as simple apartness. Purity is not excluded from the idea of the holy; it is contained within it. But the point we must remember is that the idea of the holy is never exhausted by the idea of purity. It includes purity but is much more than that. It is purity and transcendence. It is a transcendent purity.

When we use the word *holy* to describe God, we face another problem. We often describe God by compiling a list of qualities or characteristics that we call attributes. We say that God is a spirit, that He knows everything, that He is loving, just, merciful, gracious, and so on. The tendency is to add the idea of the holy to this long list of attributes as one attribute among many. But when the word *holy* is applied to God, it does not signify one single attribute. On the contrary, God is called holy in a general sense. The word is used as a synonym for His deity. That is, the word *holy* calls attention to all that God is. It reminds us that His love is holy love, His justice is holy justice, His mercy is holy mercy, His knowledge is holy knowledge, His spirit is holy spirit.

We have seen that the term *holy* calls attention to the transcendence of God, the sense in which He is above and beyond the world. We have also seen that God can reach down and consecrate special things in this world and make them holy. His touch on the common makes the common suddenly uncommon. Again we say that nothing in this world is holy in itself. Only God can make something holy. Only God can consecrate.

When we call things holy when they are not holy, we commit the sin of idolatry. We give to common things the respect, awe, worship, and adoration that belong only to God. To worship the creature instead of the Creator is the essence of idolatry.

In antiquity, idol makers were involved in a lucrative business. Some idols were made from wood, others from stone, and some from precious metals. The idol maker went to the marketplace and purchased the best materials and then went to his workshop to ply his craft. He worked long hours shaping images from the material, using his best tools and instruments. When he was finished, he swept up the floor of his workshop and carefully put his tools away in a cupboard. He then got down on his knees and started to talk to the idol he had just fashioned. Imagine talking to a dumb piece of wood or stone. The thing couldn't possibly hear what was being said. It could offer no reply. It could render no assistance. It was deaf, dumb, mute, and impotent. Yet people would ascribe holy power and worship to these objects.

Some idolaters were a bit more sophisticated. They didn't worship images of stone or totem poles. They began to worship the sun or the moon or even an abstract idea. But the sun is also a creature. There is nothing transcendent and holy about the moon. These things are all part of nature. They are all created. They may be impressive, but they do not go above and beyond the creaturely. They are not holy.

To worship an idol involves calling something holy when it is not holy. Remember, only God can consecrate. (When a minister "consecrates" a marriage or a communion wafer, it is understood that he is merely proclaiming a reality that God has already consecrated. This is an authorized use of human consecration.) When a human being tries to consecrate what God has never consecrated, it is not a genuine act of consecration. It is an act of desecration. It is an act of idolatry.

Early in the twentieth century a German scholar made an unusual and interesting study of the holy. The man's name was Rudolf Otto. Otto attempted to study the holy in a scientific way. He examined how people from different cultures and nations behave when they encounter something they regard as holy. He explored the human feelings people have when they meet the holy.

The first important discovery Otto made was that people have a difficult time describing the holy. Otto noticed that although certain things could be said about the holy, there always remained an element that defied explanation. It was not that this element was irrational. No, it was more super-rational, above the limits of our minds. There was something extra about human experience with the holy, something that could not be put into words. This is what Otto called a kind of *plus.* The plus is that part of the holy experience that people grope for words to express. It is the spiritual element that defies adequate description.

Otto coined a special term for the holy. He called it the *mysterium tremendum.* A simple translation of this concept is the "awful mystery." Otto described it like this:

> The feeling of it may at times come sweeping like a gentle tide, pervading the mind with a tranquil mood of deepest worship. It may pass over into a more set and lasting attitude of the soul, continuing, as it were, thrillingly vibrant and resonant, until at last it dies away and the soul resumes its "profane," non-religious mood of everyday experience. It may burst in sudden eruption up from the depths of the soul with spasms and convulsions, or lead to the strangest excitements, to intoxicated frenzy, to transport, and to ecstasy. It has its wild and demonic forms and can sink to an almost grisly horror and shuddering. It has its crude barbaric antecedents and early manifestations, and again it may be developed into something beautiful and pure and glorious. It may become the hushed, trembling, and speechless humility of the creature in the presence of—whom or what? In the presence of that which is a *mystery* inexpressible and above all creatures.[1]

Otto spoke of the *tremendum* (awe-fulness) because of the fear the holy provokes in us. The holy
fills us with a kind of dread. We use expressions like
"My blood ran icy cold" or "My flesh crept."

We think of the Negro spiritual: "Were you there
when they crucified my Lord?" The refrain of the
song says, "Sometimes it causes me to tremble . . .
tremble . . . tremble."

We tend to have mixed feelings about the holy.
There is a sense in which we are at the same time
attracted to it and repulsed by it. Something draws
us toward it, while at the same time we want to run
away from it. We can't seem to decide which way we
want it. Part of us yearns for the holy, while part of
us despises it. We can't live with it, and we can't live
without it.

Our attitude toward the holy is close to our attitude
toward ghost stories and horror movies. Children beg
their parents to tell them ghost stories until they get
so frightened they beg them to stop. I hate to take my
wife to scary movies. She loves to see them until she
sees them—or, I should say, doesn't see them. We go
through the same pattern each time. First she clutches
my arm and digs her fingernails into my flesh. The
only relief I get is when she removes her hands from
my arm so she can use both hands to cover her eyes.
The next step is when she leaves her seat and goes
to the rear of the theater where she can stand with
her back against a solid wall. There she can be sure
nothing is going to jump out from behind her and
grab her. The final step is when she leaves the theater
altogether and seeks refuge in the lobby. Yet she tells

me that she loves to go to such movies. (There must be a theological illustration in there somewhere.)

Perhaps the clearest example of this strange phenomenon of people's mixed feelings to the holy comes from the world of radio. Before the advent of television, the radio program was the zenith of home entertainment. We were treated to daily operas sponsored by soap companies. Duz gave us *Ma Perkins*. Other soap companies gave us *Our Gal Sunday, One Man's Family, Lorenzo Jones and His Wife, Belle*, and a host of others.

The evening programs were given to action and adventure with *The Lone Ranger, Superman, Tennessee Jed, Hop Harrigan*, and so on. My favorites were the mystery programs like *Gangbusters, The Shadow*, and *Suspense*.

The scary program of all scary programs began with the eerie sound of a creaking door opening. It sounded like fingernails scratching a blackboard. It evoked the image in my head of an ancient, musty vault being opened. With the sound of the creaking door came the sonorous voice of the announcer saying, "INNER SANCTUM!"

What is so scary about the words *inner sanctum?* What do the words mean? *Inner sanctum* simply means "within the holy." Nothing is more dreadful to us, more terrifying to the mind, than to be brought within the holy. Here we begin to tremble as we are brought into the presence of the *mysterium tremendum*.

The mysterious character of a holy God is contained in the Latin word *augustus*. The early Christians had problems giving this title to Caesar. To the Christian, no person was worthy of the title *august*. Only God could properly be called the august one. To be august is to be awe-inspiring, or awe-ful. In the ultimate sense only God is awe-ful.

In Otto's study of the human experience of the holy, he discovered that the clearest sensation that human beings have when they experience the holy is an over-powering and overwhelming sense of creatureliness. That is, when we are aware of the presence of God, we become most aware of ourselves as creatures. When we meet the Absolute, we know immediately that we are not absolute. When we meet the Infinite, we become acutely conscious that we are finite. When we meet the Eternal, we know we are temporal. To meet God is a powerful study in contrasts.

Our contrast with the "Other" is overwhelming. We think of the prophet Jeremiah and of his complaint to God: "O LORD, you deceived me, and I was deceived; you overpowered me and prevailed" (Jer. 20:7).

Here it sounds as if Jeremiah was afflicted by a bad case of stuttering. Normally the Bible is brief in its expressions, having a kind of economy of language. Jeremiah breaks the rule by taking the time to state the utterly obvious. He says, "You deceived me, and I was deceived." The last phrase is a waste of words. Of course Jeremiah was deceived. If God deceived him, how could he possibly be anything but deceived? If God overpowered him, how could he be anything but overwhelmed?

But maybe Jeremiah just wanted to make sure that God understood him when he registered his complaint. Perhaps he was using the Hebrew method of repetition to indicate emphasis. Jeremiah was deceived and overpowered. He was feeling helpless, impotent before the absolute power of God. In this moment Jeremiah was supremely aware of his own creatureliness.

Being reminded that we are creatures is not always a pleasant thing. The words of Satan's original temptation are hard to erase from our minds. "Ye shall be as gods" (Gen. 3:5, KJV). This ghastly lie of Satan's is one lie we would dearly love to be able to believe. If we could be like gods, we would be immortal, infallible, and irresistible. We would have a host of other powers that we presently do not and cannot possess.

Death often frightens us. When we see another person die, we are reminded that we are also mortal, that someday death will come to us. It is a thought we try to push from our minds. We are uncomfortable when another's death rudely intrudes into our lives and reminds us of what we will face at some unknown future date. Death reminds us that we are creatures. Yet as fearsome as death is, it is nothing compared with meeting a holy God. When we encounter Him, the totality of our creatureliness breaks upon us and shatters the myth that we have believed about ourselves, the myth that we are demigods, junior-grade deities who will try to live forever.

As mortal creatures, we are exposed to all sorts of fears. We are anxious people, given to phobias. Some people are afraid of cats, others of snakes, and still others of crowded places or lofty heights. These phobias gnaw at us and disturb our inner peace.

There is a special kind of phobia from which we all suffer. It is called *xenophobia*. Xenophobia is a fear (and sometimes a hatred) of strangers or foreigners or of anything that is strange or foreign. God is the ultimate object of our xenophobia. He is the ultimate stranger. He is the ultimate foreigner. He is holy, and we are not.

We fear God because He is holy. Our fear is not the healthy fear that the Bible encourages us to have. Our fear is a servile fear, a fear born of dread. God is too great for us; He is too awesome. He makes difficult demands on us. He is the Mysterious Stranger who threatens our security. In His presence we quake and tremble. Meeting Him personally may be our greatest trauma.

Allowing God's Holiness to Touch Our Lives

As you reflect about what you have learned and rediscovered about God's holiness, answer these questions. Use a journal to record your responses to God's holiness, or discuss your responses with a friend.

1. In what ways is God an awe-ful mystery to you?
2. Does God's mystery comfort you or frighten you?
3. What do you learn about yourself as you comprehend the mystery of God's holiness?
4. During the coming week, how will you worship God for the mystery of His holiness?

The Trauma of Holiness

Hence that dread and amazement with which,
as Scripture uniformly relates, holy men were
struck and overwhelmed whenever they beheld
the presence of God. . . . Men are never duly
touched and impressed with a conviction of their
insignificance until they have contrasted themselves
with the majesty of God.

JOHN CALVIN

It was a dark and stormy night.

I have waited for a long time to be able to begin a story with this classic expression. This introductory sentence has been so abused that some literary friends have started a club called the Dark and Stormy Night Club. Each year they present awards for the worst opening lines of books and essays.

Perhaps by the time Mark wrote his Gospel, there already was a Dark and Stormy Night Club. Notice how he begins his telling of Jesus calming the storm: "That day when evening came, he said to his disciples, 'Let us go over to the other side'" (Mark 4:35).

Jesus and His disciples were in Galilee. Jesus had been teaching the crowds who gathered on the shore of the large lake that was called the Sea of Galilee. This body of water is one of nature's grand designs. The lake fills a basin that is surrounded by mountains. Its fresh water is an important source of life to the arid countryside of Palestine.

The disciples were professional fishermen, seasoned veterans of the lake. They knew the lake's currents, its moods, and its beauty. The Sea of Galilee is like an enchanting woman whose moods are fiercely changeable. Every sailor in the region is warned of the fickleness of this body of water. Because of its peculiar location in the mountains between the Mediterranean Sea and the desert, the lake is exposed to strange quirks of nature. Violent winds can come across its surface as if they are blowing through a funnel. These winds come without warning and can turn the tranquil lake into a roaring tempest in a matter of seconds. Even with today's modern equipment, some people refuse to sail on the Sea of Galilee for fear of perishing under the wrath of the lake's violent moods.

The disciples had two things in their favor. They were veterans, and they were with the Master. When Jesus suggested that they make an evening crossing, the disciples felt no fear. They prepared their boats and made ready to cross. Then the sea had a temper tantrum; the Lady of the Lake went berserk: "A furious squall came up, and the waves broke over the boat, so that it was nearly swamped" (Mark 4:37).

The thing every Galilean fisherman feared the most happened. The unpredictable tempest hit, its violence threatening to capsize the boat. Even the strongest swimmer could not survive if hurled into the water. The men gripped the gunwales until their knuckles were white. These were crude fishing boats, not schooners or ocean liners. One sudden twist, one high wave hitting broadside could send them all to their deaths. They fought the sea furiously, trying to keep the bow into the waves. Perhaps it was here that the sailor's prayer was first uttered: "O Lord, your sea is so great, and my boat is so small."

Jesus was sound asleep in the back of the boat. He was taking a nap. I have seen similar behavior. I have been in airplanes during violent storms. I have experienced sudden losses of altitude when the plane drops like a stone for thousands of feet, leaving my stomach on the ceiling. I have heard passengers screaming in terror and seen stewardesses at the edge of panic— all while the man next to me sleeps like a baby. I've wanted to grab the fellow and shake him awake saying, "What's the matter with you? Don't you have the good sense to be scared?"

The Bible says that Jesus was sleeping on a cushion. While everybody else was in panic, Jesus was in peaceful slumber. The disciples were annoyed. Their feelings were a mixture of fear and anger. They moved to awaken Jesus. I don't know what they thought He could do about the situation. The text makes it clear that they certainly didn't expect Him to do what He did. For all intents and purposes, their situation was hopeless. The waves were getting bigger and more violent every second.

The disciples had no idea what Jesus would do. They were like people anywhere. When people are in danger, when they are threatened by peril and don't know what to do, they immediately look to their leader. It is the job of the leader to know what the next step is, even if there is no possible next step. "The disciples woke him and said to him, 'Teacher, don't you care if we drown?'" (Mark 4:38).

Their question was not really a question. It was an accusation. The suggestion was thinly veiled. They were actually saying, "You don't care if we drown." They were charging the Son of God with a lack of compassion. This outrageous attack on Jesus is consistent with mankind's customary attitude toward God. God has to listen to complaints like these from an ungrateful humanity every day. Heaven is bombarded with the repeated charges of angry people. God is called "unloving," "cruel," and "aloof," as if He has not done enough to prove His compassion for us.

There is no indication in the text that Jesus made any reply to the disciples' "question." His answer skipped over words to direct action. He saved His words for the sea and the storm:

> He got up, rebuked the wind and said to the waves, "Quiet! Be still!" Then the wind died down and it was completely calm.
>
> He said to his disciples, "Why are you so afraid? Do you still have no faith?"
> (Mark 4:39-40)

The life of Jesus was a blaze of miracles. He performed so many that it is easy for us to become jaded in the hearing of them. We can read this narrative and skip quickly over to the next page without being moved. Yet we have here one of the most astonishing of all Jesus' miracles. We have an event that made a special impression on the disciples. It was a miracle that was mind boggling, even to them.

Jesus controlled the fierce forces of nature by the sound of His voice. He didn't say a prayer. He didn't ask the Father to deliver them from the tempest. He dealt with the situation directly. He uttered a command, a divine imperative. Instantly nature obeyed. The wind heard the voice of its Creator. The sea recognized the command of its Lord. Instantly the wind ceased. Not a zephyr could be felt in the air. The sea became like glass, without the tiniest ripple.

Notice the reaction of the disciples. The sea was now calm, but they were still agitated: "They were terrified and asked each other, 'Who is this? Even the wind and the waves obey him!'" (Mark 4:41).

We see a strange pattern unfolding here. That the storm and raging sea frightened the disciples is not surprising. But once the danger passed and the sea was calm, it would seem that their fear would vanish as suddenly as the storm. It didn't happen that way. Now that the sea was calm, the fear of the disciples *increased*. How do we account for that?

It was the father of modern psychiatry, Sigmund Freud, who once espoused the theory that people invent religion out of a fear of nature. We feel helpless before an earthquake, a flood, or a ravaging disease. So, said Freud, we invent a God who has power over the earthquake, flood, and disease. God is personal. We can talk to Him. We can try to bargain with Him. We can plead with Him to save us from the destructive forces of nature. We are not able to plead with earthquakes, negotiate with floods, or bargain with cancer. So, the theory goes, we invent God to help us deal with these scary things.

What is significant about this scriptural story is that the disciples' fear increased after the threat of the storm was removed. The storm had made them afraid. Jesus' action to still the tempest made them more afraid. In the power of Christ they met something more frightening than they had ever met in nature. They were in the presence of the holy. We wonder what Freud would have said about that. Why would the disciples invent a God whose holiness was more terrifying than the forces of nature that provoked them to invent a god in the first place? We can understand it if people invented an unholy god, a god who brought only comfort. But why a god more scary than the earthquake, flood, or disease? It is one thing to fall victim to the flood or to fall prey to cancer; *it is another thing to fall into the hands of the living God.*

The words that the disciples spoke after Jesus calmed the sea are very revealing. They cried out, "Who is this?" The King James Version expresses the question like this: "What manner of man is this, that even the wind and the sea obey him?" The question was "What *manner* of man is this?" They were asking a question of *kind.* They were looking for a category to put Jesus in, a category with which they were familiar. If we can classify people into certain types, we know immediately how to deal with them. We respond one way to hostile people and another way to friendly people. We react one way to intellectual types and another way to social types. The disciples could find no category adequate to capture the person of Jesus. He was beyond typecasting. He was *sui generis*—in a class by Himself.

The disciples had never met a man like this. He was one of a kind, a complete foreigner. They had met all different kinds of men before—tall men, short men, fat men, skinny men, smart men, and stupid men. They had met Greeks, Romans, Syrians, Egyptians, Samaritans, and fellow Jews. But they had never met a holy man, a man who could speak to wind and waves and have them obey Him.

That Jesus could sleep through the storm at sea was strange enough. But it was not unique. I think again of my fellow airplane passenger who dozed while I was gripped with panic. It may be rare to meet people who can slumber through a crisis, but it is not unprecedented. I was impressed with my friend on the plane. But he did not awaken and yell out the window to the wind and make it stop at his command. If he had done that, I would have looked around for a parachute.

Jesus was different. He possessed an awesome otherness. He was the supreme mysterious stranger. He made people uncomfortable.

The account of Christ calming the storm had a kind of instant replay in Jesus' ministry. Luke gives the setting as the Lake of Gennesaret. It seems that at times the Jews had trouble making up their minds what to call the large body of water nestled in the hills of Galilee. The Lake of Gennesaret was one and the same body of water that is elsewhere called the Sea of Galilee.

> One day as Jesus was standing by the Lake of Gennesaret, with the people crowding around him and listening to the word of God, he saw at the water's edge two boats, left there by the fishermen, who were washing their nets. He

got into one of the boats, the one belonging to Simon, and asked him to put out a little from shore. Then he sat down and taught the people from the boat.

When he had finished speaking, he said to Simon, "Put out into deep water, and let down the nets for a catch."

Simon answered, "Master, we've worked hard all night and haven't caught anything. But because you say so, I will let down the nets."

When they had done so, they caught such a large number of fish that their nets began to break. So they signaled their partners in the other boat to come and help them, and they came and filled both boats so full that they began to sink. (Luke 5:1-7)

If ever there was a time when the disciples displayed annoyance and irritation with Jesus, this was the occasion. Simon Peter was tired. He had been up all night and was frustrated by the lack of success in his fishing. The catch had been terrible. Such an experience was enough to put a professional fisherman in a foul mood. Add to his weariness the additional frustration of dealing with the multitudes who were pushing around him all morning as Jesus was teaching. When Jesus' sermon was finished, Simon was ready to go home and go to bed. But Jesus wanted to go fishing. He had a marvelous idea about casting out into the deep water.

It doesn't require a lot of imagination to read between the lines and catch Simon's seething sarcasm. "Master, we've worked hard all night and haven't caught anything. But because you say so, I will let down the nets." Real respect for the wisdom of Jesus in this circumstance would have had Simon saying, simply, "I will let down the nets." Instead, he found it necessary to register his frustration. It is as if he said, "Look, Jesus, you are a marvelous teacher. Your words keep us all spellbound. In matters of religion you confound us all. But, please, give us a little bit of credit. We are professionals. We know the fishing business. We have been out there all night and nothing—zilch. The fish just aren't running. Let's go home, go to bed, and try again later. But if you insist, if we must humor you, then, of course we will let down the nets."

I can see Simon Peter exchanging a knowing glance with Andrew and muttering complaints under his breath as he hoisted the nets that he had just cleaned and threw them overboard. He must have been thinking to himself, *Blasted teachers! They're all alike. They think they know everything.*

We know how it turned out. No sooner had Peter dropped the nets where Jesus told him, than it seemed as if every fish in the Lake of Gennesaret jumped into them. It was as if the fish were having a contest to see who could jump in first. "Last one in is a rotten eel!"

So many fish filled the nets that the strain was too great. The nets began to break. When the other disciples rushed to the scene with their boat, it was still not enough. Both boats were so filled to the brim with fish that the vessels began to sink. This was the most extraordinary catch the fishermen had ever witnessed.

How did Peter react? How would you have reacted? I know what I would have done. I would have pulled out a contract on the spot. I would have asked Jesus to show up at the dock once a month for five minutes. I would have owned the most lucrative fishing business in history.

Business and profits were the things furthest from Peter's mind. When the nets were bursting, Peter couldn't even see the fish. All he could see was Jesus. Hear what he said: "When Simon Peter saw this, he fell at Jesus' knees and said, 'Go away from me, Lord; I am a sinful man!'" (Luke 5:8).

At that moment Peter realized that he was in the presence of the Holy Incarnate. He was desperately uncomfortable. His initial response was one of worship. He fell to his knees before Christ. Instead of saying something like, "Lord, I adore you, I magnify you," he said, "Please go away. Please leave. I can't stand it."

The history of the life of Christ is a history of multitudes of people pushing through crowds just to get close to Him. It is the leper crying, "Have mercy on me." It is the woman who had been bleeding for twelve years reaching out to touch the hem of His garment. It is the thief on the cross straining to hear Jesus' dying words. It is people saying, "Come close to me. Look at me. Touch me."

Not so Peter. His anguished plea was different: He asked Jesus to depart, to give him space, to leave him alone.

Why? We need not speculate here. It is not necessary to read between the lines because the lines themselves state precisely why Peter wanted Jesus gone: "I am a sinful man!" Sinful people are not comfortable in the presence of the holy. The cliché is that misery loves company. Another is that there is fellowship among thieves. But thieves do not seek the consoling presence of the fellowship of police officers. Sinful misery does not love the company of purity.

We notice that Jesus did not lecture Peter about his sins. There was no rebuke, no word of judgment. All Jesus did was to show Peter how to catch fish. But when the holy is manifest, no words are needed to express it. Peter got a message that was impossible to miss. The transcendent standard of all righteousness and all purity blazed before his eyes. Like Isaiah before him, Peter was undone.

One of the strange facts of history is the consistently good reputation Jesus of Nazareth enjoys even with unbelievers. It is rare for an unbeliever to speak unkindly of Jesus. People who are openly hostile to the church and who hold Christians in contempt are often unsparing in their praise for Jesus. Even Friedrich Nietzsche, who announced the death of God and lamented the decadence of the church, spoke of Jesus as a model of the heroic. In the final years of his life, which were spent in a lunatic asylum, Nietzsche expressed his own insanity by signing his letters, "The Crucified One."

The overwhelming testimony of the world is to the incomparable perfection of Jesus. Even George Bernard Shaw, when critical of Jesus, could think of no higher standard than Christ Himself. He said of Jesus,

"There were times when he did not behave as a Christian." We cannot miss the irony of Shaw's criticism.

In terms of moral excellence, even those who do not ascribe to the deity or saviorhood of Christ applaud Jesus the man. Like Pontius Pilate they declare, *"Ecce homo."* "Behold the man!" "I find no fault in Him."

With all the applause Jesus gets, it seems difficult to understand why His contemporaries killed Him. Why did the multitudes scream for His blood? Why did the Pharisees loathe Him? Why was such a nice, upright fellow condemned to death by the highest religious court in the land?

To understand this mystery we might look to modern-day Palestine for an answer. The pilgrim who visits Jerusalem is stunned by the magnificence of the venerable city. At night the ancient walls are bathed by floodlights, giving a magical look to the Holy City. If one approaches the city from the Mount of Olives and passes through the Valley of Kidron along the winding road, he or she will see the standing memorial of the Tomb of the Prophets adorning the roadway along the Eastern Wall near the pinnacle of the temple. The memorial has been standing there for centuries, dating all the way back to the time of Christ. There, in bold relief, are the sculpted figures of the great prophets of the Old Testament, like a Jewish miniature Mount Rushmore.

In Jesus' day the Old Testament prophets were venerated. They were the great folk heroes from the past. Yet when they were alive they were hated, scorned, rejected, despised, persecuted, and killed by their contemporaries.

Stephen was the first Christian martyr. He was killed by a furious mob because he reminded his audience of the blood that was on their hands:

> You stiff-necked people, with uncircumcised hearts and ears! You are just like your fathers: You always resist the Holy Spirit! Was there ever a prophet your fathers did not persecute? They even killed those who predicted the coming of the Righteous One. And now you have betrayed and murdered him—you who have received the law that was put into effect through angels but have not obeyed it. (Acts 7:51-53)

We might expect that these stinging words from Stephen would have pierced the hearts of his hearers and led them to repentance. But such was not the effect: "When they heard this, they were furious and gnashed their teeth at him. . . . At this they covered their ears and, yelling at the top of their voices, they all rushed at him, dragged him out of the city and began to stone him" (Acts 7:54, 57-58).

People have an appreciation for moral excellence, as long as it is removed a safe distance from them. The Jews honored the prophets, from a distance. The world honors Christ, from a distance.

Peter wanted to be with Jesus, until He got too close. Then Peter cried, "Please leave."

In the 1970s, the book *The Peter Principle* by Laurence Peter and Raymond Hull reached the top of the best-seller lists. The fundamental point of its teaching has since become an axiom in the business world: that people tend to rise to their level of incompetence in the corporate structures. The Peter Principle has nothing to do with Simon Peter except that it partially explains why Peter was uncomfortable in the presence of Jesus.

The Peter Principle involves the questions of competence and incompetence. The axiom that people tend to rise to the level of their incompetence is based on a study of promotions in the business world. When people do well, they are promoted. They rise up a notch in the organization. Their upward climb is finally arrested at a certain point. It is the point where they cease to do well. When they stop doing well, they stop getting promoted and are doomed to spend the rest of their days working at a level that is one step above their level of competency. People get locked into their level of incompetency, a tragedy for them and for their companies.

Not everyone gets caught in the trap of the Peter Principle. Authors Peter and Hull mention two categories of people who escape the trap: the super-incompetent and the super-competent. The super-incompetent people have no opportunity to move up to their level of incompetence because they are already incompetent. There is no level at which they are competent. They are incompetent at the lowest level of the organization. These people are weeded out of the organization early.

The real irony is found in the other group that "escapes" the Peter Principle. This group is that of the super-competent. How do super-competent people rise through the corporate structures to get to the top? They don't. The book asserts that the great difficulty super-competent people have in rising up the corporate ladder is that they represent a massive threat to those above them. Their bosses are frightened by them, fearful that they will displace them. Super-competent people represent a clear and present danger that their superiors will lose their seats of honor and power. Super-competent people succeed not by moving up the organizational ladder but also by making jumping moves from one organization to another, moving higher up as they go.

It is easy for us to dismiss Peter and Hull's theory as pure cynicism. We can point to countless examples of people who have had meteoric rises in companies and reached the very top. More than one chief executive officer started in the company as a clerk. Peter and Hull would reply, of course, that these dramatic Horatio Alger stories are the exceptions that prove the rule.

Whatever the true statistics are, the indisputable fact remains that there are numerous occasions where super-competent people are frozen at a low level because they threaten those above them. Not everyone applauds success. I remember a senior student I had in my college teaching days. She was the best female student I had ever had. Her cumulative average was a solid 4.0. Her work was extraordinary.

I was shocked when I graded one of her senior exams, which she flunked miserably. Her performance was such a radical departure from her normal level that I knew something was seriously wrong. I called her into my office for a meeting and asked her what went wrong. She immediately burst into tears and between sobs confessed that she had intentionally failed the exam. When I asked her why, she explained that as she was nearing graduation, she was experiencing a growing fear that she would never find a husband. "None of the guys want to date me," she said. "They all think that I'm too smart, that I'm just a brain." She poured out a heart-wrenching tale of loneliness and a personal feeling of being ostracized from the social life on campus. She was feeling like a pariah.

This student had committed the socially unpardonable sin. She had broken the curve. I know what it means to grade on a curve both from the vantage point of the student and of the teacher. I remember my student days and the dreadful feeling of walking out of a classroom after doing poorly on a test. I remember how it was music to my ears when teachers said that they would grade the test on a curve. That meant if I got only 60 percent on the test, the curve might promote me from a D to a C, or even to a B if enough people did poorly. This put me in a position where I was rooting for the other students to fail.

But there was always one in the crowd. When everyone else was making 20s and 30s on the test, giving incontrovertible evidence that the test was unfair, and the teacher would be morally bound to grade by the curve, there was the inevitable brain who would make 100 percent on the test. I can't ever recall the students rising to their feet to offer the brain a standing ovation. Nobody likes curve breakers. They make us all look bad.

Jesus Christ was a curve breaker. He was the supreme curve buster. He was the ultimate super-competent. The outcasts of society loved Him because He paid attention to them. But those who held the seats of honor and power could not tolerate Christ.

The party of the Jews who declared themselves the mortal enemies of Jesus were the Pharisees.

The Pharisees traced their beginnings to the period of history between the close of the Old Testament period and the beginning of the New Testament period. The sect was started by men who had a great zeal for the Law. The word *Pharisee* literally meant "one who is separated." The Pharisees separated themselves unto holiness. The pursuit of holiness was the chief business of their lives. They majored in holiness. If any group should have thrown their hats in the air when the holy appeared on the scene, it was the Pharisees.

Through their singular devotion to the pursuit of holiness, the Pharisees achieved a level of popular respect for piety and righteousness that was without parallel. They had no peers. They were accorded lofty human praise. They were welcomed to privileged seats in the banquet halls. They were admired as experts in religion. Their uniforms were decorated with the tassels of their exalted ranks. They could be seen practicing their virtue in public places. They fasted where everyone could see them. They bowed their heads in solemn prayer on the street corners and restaurants. No one missed the clang of the coin in the beggar's cup when the Pharisees gave alms. Their "holiness" was plain for everyone to see.

Jesus called them hypocrites. ·

Jesus pronounced upon them the prophetic oracle of doom: "Woe to you, teachers of the law and Pharisees, you hypocrites! You travel over land and sea to win a single convert, and when he becomes one, you make him twice as much a son of hell as you are" (Matt. 23:15). Jesus' denunciation of the Pharisees was severe. He criticized them for several counts of hypocrisy. Let us examine a few of the charges Jesus brought against them:

> The teachers of the law and the Pharisees sit in Moses' seat. So you must obey them and do everything they tell you. But do not do what they do, for they do not practice what they preach. They tie up heavy loads and put them on men's shoulders, but they themselves are not willing to lift a finger to move them.

> Everything they do is done for men to see: They make their phylacteries wide and the tassels on their garments long; they love the place of honor at banquets and the most important seats in the synagogues; they love to be greeted in the marketplaces and to have men call them "Rabbi." (Matt. 23:2-7)

There was no understated elegance about the Pharisees. There was no authentic beauty to their holiness. They were showy and ostentatious in their outward displays. Their holiness was a sham. The hypocrite was a playactor of righteousness:

> Woe to you, teachers of the law and Pharisees, you hypocrites! You clean the outside of the cup and dish, but inside they are full of greed and self-indulgence. Blind Pharisee! First clean the inside of the cup and dish, and then the outside also will be clean.

> Woe to you, teachers of the law and Pharisees, you hypocrites! You are like whitewashed tombs, which look beautiful on the outside but on the inside are full of dead men's bones and everything unclean. In the same way, on the outside you appear to people as righteous but on the inside you are full of hypocrisy and wickedness. (Matt. 23:25-28)

The images Jesus used are striking. He pictures the Pharisees as being like cups that are clean only on the outside. Imagine going to a restaurant and having the waiter put a cup in front of you that is sparkling clean on the outside but is filled with the residue of yesterday's coffee grounds on the inside of the cup. It would do little to enhance your appetite. So was the service of the Pharisees. As whitewashed tombs conceal the grisly truth of bodily decomposition and putrefying flesh, so the facade of the Pharisees hid from view the rottenness of their souls.

Consider for a moment a few brief epithets that Jesus reserved for the Pharisees: "You snakes!" "You brood of vipers!" "Blind guides!" "Sons of hell!" "Blind fools!" These forms of address can hardly be considered compliments. Jesus spared no invectives in His denunciations of these men. His words were uncharacteristically harsh, though not unjustifiably harsh. They were different from His usual style. The normal form of rebuke He made to sinners was gentle. He spoke tenderly, though firmly, to the woman caught in adultery and to the woman at the well. It seems that Jesus saved His severe comments for the big boys, the theological professionals. With them He asked no quarter and gave none.

We might argue that the Pharisees hated Jesus because He was so critical of them. No one likes to be criticized, especially people who are accustomed to praise. But the venom of the Pharisees went deeper than that. It is safe to assume that had Jesus said nothing to them, they still would have despised Him. His mere presence was enough to cause them to recoil from Him.

It has been said that nothing dispels a lie faster than the truth; nothing exposes the counterfeit faster than the genuine. Clever counterfeit dollars may be unnoticed by the untrained eye. What every counterfeiter fears is that someone will examine his bogus bill while holding a genuine one next to it. The presence of Jesus represented the presence of the genuine in the midst of the bogus. Here authentic holiness appeared; the counterfeiters of holiness were not pleased.

The Sadducees had the same problem with Jesus. They were the exalted priestly class of the day. They took their name from the Old Testament priest Zadok, whose name, in turn, was taken from the Jewish word for "righteous." If the Pharisees considered themselves to be the holy ones, the Sadducees claimed to be the righteous ones. With the appearance of Jesus, their righteousness took on the luster of unrighteousness. Their curve was broken too.

The resentment of the Pharisees and Sadducees toward Jesus began as a petty annoyance, moved to the level of a smoldering rage, and finally exploded in vehement demands for His death. They simply could not tolerate Him. On the Sea of Galilee the disciples were unable to find a category fitting for Christ; they could not answer their own question, "What manner of man is this?" The Pharisees and the Sadducees had a ready answer. They created categories for Jesus: He was a "blasphemer" and a "devil." He had to go. The super-competent had to be destroyed.

The incarnate Christ is no longer walking the earth. He has ascended into heaven. No one sees Him or speaks audibly with Him in the flesh today. Yet the threatening power of His holiness is still felt. Sometimes it is transferred to His people. As the Jews at the foot of Mount Sinai fled in terror from the dazzling face of Moses, so people today get uncomfortable in the mere presence of Christians.

Struggling with the Dutch language was one of the most difficult aspects of my education. When I went to Holland to study, I was bewildered by this language that had such a lilting sound to it. Its vowel sounds were almost impossible for me to pronounce, and the language was rich in strange idioms. Just when

I would think that I had the language under control, I would hear an expression that totally mystified me.

Such was the expression I heard at a dinner party at a friend's house in Amsterdam. The conversation was animated until suddenly there was a gap, an unplanned break in the conversation that brought with it a brief awkward silence. To break the silence, one of my Dutch friends said, *"Er gaat een Domine voorbij!"* I replied, "What did you say?" The strange phrase was repeated. I knew what the words meant, but the expression made no sense. To break the awkward silence, he had said, "A minister walked by!"

Again I asked my friends for an explanation. They explained that it was a custom in Holland to use this expression whenever an awkward silence threatened a lively conversation. To say that a minister walked by was to offer an explanation for the sudden silence. The idea was that nothing could ruin the conviviality of a party faster than the presence of a clergyman. When the minister appears, the fun is over. There can be no more laughter, no more lively conversation, only a stilted silence. When such silences came, the only explanation could be that a minister had just walked by.

I experience the same phenomenon frequently on the golf course. If I get paired with strangers, everything goes fine until they ask me what I do. As soon as they find out I am a clergyman, the whole atmosphere changes. They begin to stand farther away from me as we speak, giving me extra space. It is as if they suddenly realize that I have some dreadful disease, and it might be contagious. Profuse apologies usually follow regarding their language. "I'm sorry for swearing. I didn't know that you were a minister." As if the minister never heard such words before or that it was unthinkable that in his whole life such words had ever passed over his lips. The Isaiah-complex of the dirty mouth is still with us.

Scripture says that "the wicked flee when no one pursues" (Prov. 28:1, NKJV). Luther stated it this way, "The pagan trembles at the rustling of a leaf." The uncomfortable feeling that is provoked by the presence of clergymen is fallout from the identification of the church with Christ. It can have strange effects on people.

In the 1970s, one of the leading golfers on the professional tour was invited to play in a foursome with Gerald Ford (then president of the United States), Jack Nicklaus, and Billy Graham. The golfer was especially in awe of playing with Ford and Billy Graham (he had played frequently with Nicklaus before).

After the round of golf was finished, one of the other pros came up to the golfer and asked, "Hey, what was it like playing with the president and with Billy Graham?"

The pro unleashed a torrent of cursing, and in a disgusted manner said, "I don't need Billy Graham stuffing religion down my throat." With that he turned on his heel and stormed off, heading for the practice tee.

His friend followed the angry pro to the practice tee. The pro took out his driver and started to beat out balls in fury. His neck was crimson, and it looked as if steam was coming from his ears. His friend said nothing. He sat on a bench and watched. After a few minutes the anger of the pro was spent. He settled down. His friend said quietly, "Was Billy a little rough on you out there?"

The pro heaved an embarrassed sigh and said, "No, he didn't even mention religion. I just had a bad round."

Astonishing. Billy Graham had said not a word about God, Jesus, or religion, yet the pro had stormed away after the game accusing Billy of trying to ram religion down his throat. How can we explain this? It's really not difficult. Billy Graham didn't have to say a word; he didn't have to give a single sideward glance to make the pro feel uncomfortable. Billy Graham is so identified with religion, so associated with the things of God, that his very presence is enough to smother the wicked person who flees when no one pursues. Luther was right, pagans do tremble at the rustling of a leaf. They feel the hound of heaven breathing down their neck. They feel crowded by holiness, even if it is made present only by an imperfect, partially sanctified human vessel.

The golf pro's reaction to Billy Graham was similar to Peter's reaction to Jesus Christ. "Go away from me, Lord; I am a sinful man!" Both felt the trauma of the presence of the holy. Holiness provokes hatred. The greater the holiness, the greater the human hostility toward it. It seems insane. No man was ever more loving than Jesus Christ. Yet even His love made people angry. His love was a perfect love, a transcendent and holy love, but His very love brought trauma to people. This kind of love is so majestic we can't stand it.

A well-known story in American literature describes a kind of love that destroys. It is a freakish love, a love so intense that it crushes the object of its affection. Students of the writing of John Steinbeck have suggested that his famous character Lennie, in *Of Mice and Men,* was in fact a Christ figure.

Lennie a Christ figure? Many Christians are offended by the suggestion. Lennie is a big, dumb brute. He is a murderer. How could such a person ever serve as a Christ figure?

Of Mice and Men is the story of two migrant workers, Lennie and George, who wander over the countryside from job to job, dreaming of the day when they can own their own farm. Steinbeck describes them:

> Both were dressed in denim trousers and in denim coats with brass buttons. Both wore black, shapeless hats, and both carried tight blanket rolls slung over their shoulders. The first man was small and quick, dark of face, with restless eyes and sharp, strong features. Every part of him was defined: small, strong hands, slender arms, a thin and bony nose. Behind him walked his opposite, a huge man, shapeless of face, with large, pale eyes, with wide sloping shoulders; and he walked heavily, dragging his feet a little, the way a bear drags his paws. His arms did not swing at his sides but hung loosely.

Notice the contrast in the two characters. George's face is clearly defined. Lennie is "shapeless of face." There is something incomprehensible about this hulk of a man. He walks like a bear, but he has the mind of a naive child. Lennie is mentally retarded. He is virtually helpless without George. George has to take care of him and speak to him in the simplest of terms.

Lennie has a strange quirk. He loves little furry animals—mice, rabbits, and the like. He dreams of the day when George will get their farm and he can keep rabbits and mice of his own. But Lennie has a problem. He doesn't understand his own strength. When he picks up a field mouse or a rabbit, all he wants to do is love it, to shower his affection on it. But the furry creatures don't understand. They are frightened and try to escape Lennie's grasp. Lennie squeezes them so he can hold them still to receive his love. Unintentionally he kills them, squeezing the life out of them with his heavy hands.

Lennie's preoccupation with little furry creatures is a constant source of annoyance to George. He gets upset when he discovers that Lennie is walking around with a dead mouse in his jacket pocket. The thing is rank. But George loves Lennie like a son and patiently abides these foibles. The climax of the book comes when Lennie finds himself alone with the foreman's wife:

> Curley's wife laughed at him. "You're nuts," she said. "But you're a kinda nice fella. Jus' like a big baby. But a person can see kinda what you mean. When I'm doin' my hair sometimes I jus' set an' stroke it 'cause it's so soft." To show how

she did it, she ran her fingers over the top of her head. "Some people got kinda coarse hair," she said complacently. "Take Curley. His hair is jus' like wire. But mine is soft and fine. 'Course I brush it a lot. That makes it fine. Here—feel right here." She took Lennie's hand and put it on her head. "Feel right aroun' there an' see how soft it is."

Lennie's big fingers fell to stroking her hair.

"Don't you muss it up," she said.

Lennie said, "Oh! That's nice," and he stroked harder. "Oh, that's nice."

"Look out, now, you'll muss it." And then she cried angrily, "You stop it now, you'll mess it all up." She jerked her head sideways, and Lennie's fingers closed on her hair and hung on. "Let go," she cried. "You let go!"

Lennie was in a panic. His face was contorted. She screamed then, and Lennie's other hand closed over her mouth and nose. "Please don't," he begged. "Oh! Please don't do that. George'll be mad."

She struggled violently under his hands. Her feet battered on the hay and she writhed to be free; and from under Lennie's hand came a muffled scream. Lennie began to cry with fright. "Oh! Please don't do none of that," he begged. "George gonna say I done a bad thing. He ain't gonna let me tend no rabbits."

He moved his hand a little and her hoarse cry came out. Then Lennie grew angry. "Now don't," he said, "I don't want you to yell. You gonna get me in trouble jus' like George says you will. Now don't you do that." And she continued to struggle, and her eyes were wild with terror. He shook her then, and he was angry with her. "Don't you go yellin'," he said, and he shook her; and her body flopped like a fish. And then she was still, for Lennie had broken her neck.

It was one thing for Lennie to kill mice, quite another to kill people. This time his strange quirk had gone too far. George led Lennie away, fleeing into the countryside from the pursuing posse. They reached the edge of a deep green pool of the Salinas River. They sat down to rest and began to talk. Lennie waited for George to scold him for doing a bad thing. Then Lennie asked George to tell him again about the farm they would own someday.

Lennie said, "Tell how it's gonna be." George had been listening to the distant sounds. For a moment he was businesslike. "Look acrost the river, Lennie, an' I'll tell you so you can almost see it."

Lennie turned his head and looked off across the pool and up the darkening slopes of the Gabilans. "We gonna get a little place," George began.

While Lennie was locked in reverie, seeing in the distance the longed-for farm, George took a Luger out of his pocket. Lennie's attention was riveted on the imaginary rabbits and chickens that were dancing in front of his eyes. As the posse came closer, George took aim and pulled the trigger.

Slim, the leader of the posse, was the first at the scene.

> He went over and looked down at Lennie, and then he looked back at George. "Right in the back of the head," he said softly.
>
> Slim came directly to George and sat down beside him, sat very close to him. "Never you mind," said Slim. "A guy got to sometimes."

"A guy got to sometimes." Sometimes people have to be executed, people who are destructive. People who crush other people cannot be tolerated. Never mind that the force behind Lennie's destructive acts was a force of childlike, innocent love. His love had no ulterior motives, no hint of seduction. His was a pure love; a love so intense that it strangled people who resisted it. George had no alternative. He knew Lennie could not survive in this world. Lennie had to die. Lennie traumatized everyone and everything he touched.

So it was with Christ. The world could tolerate Jesus; they could love Him, but only at a distance. Christ is safe for us if securely bound by space and time. But a present Christ could not survive in a world of hostile men. It was the judgment of Caiaphas that, for the good of the nation, Jesus must die. Sometimes ya just got to.

Allowing God's Holiness to Touch Our Lives

As you reflect about what you have learned and redis-covered about God's holiness, answer these questions. Use a journal to record your responses to God's holi-ness, or discuss your responses with a friend.

1. Is your view of God's holiness like Peter's? Do you want to run from it?
2. Have you ever experienced the trauma of God's holiness?
3. Describe a time when you were comforted by God's holiness.
4. Of what aspect of God's holiness were you most aware this past week?

CHAPTER FIVE

The Insanity of Luther

Let God be God.

MARTIN LUTHER

If we fix our minds on the holiness of God, the result might be disturbing. Martin Luther's spirit was troubled by a deep knowledge of the character of God. Luther's unusual personality was shaped in part by his study of God. Was his personality enhanced or distorted? Was his spirit purified or demented by his encounter with God?

"Love God? Sometimes I hate Him." This is a strange quote to hear from the lips of a man as respected for his religious zeal as Luther. But he said it. He was noted for making outrageous statements. "Sometimes Christ seems to me nothing more than an angry judge who comes to me with a sword in His hand."

Was the man crazy? Before we try to answer that question, let us examine some of the features of Luther's life and behavior that have prompted the judgment that he was, in fact, insane.

The first key to Luther's profile is found in his tempestuous outbursts of anger and his intemperate language. He was fond of calling his critics "dogs." "The dogs are starting to bark," he would say when reactions from his critics reached his ears. His language was at times earthy, salted with scatological references.

Consider an example of Luther's reply to the diatribe of Erasmus:

> It seemed a complete waste of time to reply to your arguments. I have already myself refuted them over and over again, and Philip Melancthon, in his unsurpassed volume on the doctrines of theology, has trampled them in the dust. That book of his, to my mind, deserves not merely to live as long as books are read, but to take its place in the Church's canon; whereas your book, by comparison, struck me as so worthless and poor that my heart went out to you for having defiled your lovely, brilliant flow of language with such vile stuff. I thought it outrageous to convey material of so low a quality in the trappings of such rare eloquence; it is like using gold or silver dishes to carry garden rubbish or dung.[1]

Luther's tempestuous behavior came to the surface in an important meeting at Marburg. Leaders of the new Protestant movement came together to iron out disagreements about the Lord's Supper. In the midst of the dialogue Luther began to pound his fist on the table, saying over and over again, *"Hoc est corpus meum, hoc est corpus meum."* ("This is my body.") His antics were similar to the shoe-banging tantrum made famous by Nikita Khrushchev at the United Nations.

Luther was unquestionably intemperate at times. He was given to bombast. His insults, calling people dogs, were often severe. But these issues, though enough to raise questions about his propriety, are hardly matters that bear on his sanity.

But there is more to the matter than Luther's speech patterns. His behavior was at times downright bizarre. He was afflicted by an assortment of phobias. A well-known story recalls that Luther was walking in the midst of a severe thunderstorm when a bolt of lightning crashed so close to him that he was thrown to the ground. The great church historian and biographer of Luther, Roland Bainton, tells the story:

> On a sultry day in July of the year 1505 a lonely traveler was trudging over a parched road on the outskirts of the Saxon village of Stotternheim. He was a young man, short but sturdy, and wore the dress of a university student. As he approached the village, the sky became overcast. Suddenly there was a shower, then a crashing storm. A bolt of lightning rived the gloom and knocked the man to the ground. Struggling to rise, he cried in terror, "St. Anne, help me! I will become a monk."

> The man who thus called upon a saint was later to repudiate the cult of saints. He who vowed to become a monk was later to renounce monasticism. A loyal son of the Catholic Church, he was later to shatter the structure of medieval catholicism. A devoted servant of the pope, he was later to identify the

popes with Antichrist. For this young man was Martin Luther.[2]

Shortly after this experience, Luther paid his vow. He quit his studies in law and entered the monastery, much to the dismay of his father, Hans.

The fear of violent death as an expression of divine judgment and punishment haunted Luther. He suffered from stomach ailments throughout his life as well as from kidney stones, a most painful malady. On more than one occasion he predicted his death. Numerous times he was sure that he was only days or weeks away from the grave. The lightning bolt seared in his memory a scar that he never forgot.

Not everyone reacts the same way to a close brush with death from lightning. On June 27, 1975, three professional golfers were knocked to the ground by a lightning bolt during the Western Open near Chicago. One of the three, Lee Trevino, suffered a back injury that severely hampered his future career. When interviewed on a television talk show about the incident, the host inquired of Trevino, "What did you learn from the experience?"

In typical "Merry Mex" fashion Trevino replied, "I learned that if the Almighty wants to play through, you better get out of His way." Then he added, "I should have been holding a 1-iron over my head during the storm."

The host was puzzled by this cryptic statement and bit. "Why is that?" he asked.

Trevino's eyes twinkled, and he quipped, "Because not even God can hit a 1-iron."

Trevino gained some jokes for his repertoire from his experience. Luther gained a new career as a monk and a theologian.

Luther's chronic stomach troubles have also been linked to a psychosomatic problem. His neurotic phobias all seemed to go directly to his stomach, destroying his digestion. His problem with flatulence has become legendary, due in part to his own exaggeration of it. His writings are sprinkled with references to his constant belching and breaking of wind. He said, "If I break wind in Wittenburg, they will hear it in Leipzig."

Fortunately Luther was able to find a sanctified use for his flatulence. He advised his students that the breaking of wind was a most effective device to repel the attacks of the devil. Elsewhere Luther spoke of resisting Satan by throwing an inkwell at him. Luther described his battle with Satan in the terms of a man under siege. He was sure that he was a personal target of the prince of hell.

The Satan stories are ripe with fodder for practicing psychologists, who see in these accounts two indications of mental imbalance. On the one hand Luther is thought to have suffered from hallucinations, and on the other from delusions of grandeur that the prince of darkness would single him out as his favorite target.

Yet from the vantage point of church history, it should not surprise us to think that in the sixteenth century, satanic energy might most strongly be focused on Martin Luther.

Another episode that has caused psychiatrists to

raise their eyebrows was the celebration of Luther's first mass. Luther had distinguished himself already as a budding theologian and was not shy. His future as a dramatic pulpiteer and master public orator was still unknown to his contemporaries.

The celebration of his first mass following his ordination was Luther's public debut as a cleric. Old Hans Luther had almost made his peace with his son's decision to give up a lucrative career in law in favor of the monastic life. He was feeling some pride—"My son, the priest." The scheduled celebration was seen as a time for family pride, and Luther's relatives joined the public to observe his celebration.

None in attendance expected what happened. Luther began the ceremony with great poise, exuding a priestly bearing of confidence and self-control. When he came to the Prayer of Consecration—that moment in the mass when Luther would exercise his priestly authority for the first time to evoke the power of God to perform the great miracle of transubstantiation (the changing of the elements of bread and wine to the real body and blood of Christ)—Luther faltered.

He froze at the altar. He seemed transfixed. His eyes were glassy, and beads of perspiration formed on his forehead. A nervous hush filled the congregation as they silently urged the young priest on. Hans Luther was growing uncomfortable, feeling a wave of parental embarrassment sweep over him. His son's lower lip began to quiver. He was trying to speak the words of the mass, but no words came forth from his mouth. He went limp and returned to the table where his father and the family guests were seated. He had

failed. He had ruined the mass and disgraced himself
and his father. Hans was furious. He had just made a
generous contribution to the monastery and now felt
humiliated in the very place he came to witness his
son's honor. He lashed out at Martin and questioned
whether his son was fit to be a priest. Martin defended
his calling by appealing to the heavenly summons he
felt in the lightning-bolt experience. Hans rejoined,
"God grant it was not an apparition of the devil."

What happened at the altar? Luther offers his own
explanation at the paralysis that struck when he was
supposed to say the words, "We offer unto thee, the
living, the true, the eternal God." He said:

> At these words I was utterly stupefied and
> terror-stricken. I thought to myself, "With
> what tongue shall I address such majesty,
> seeing that all men ought to tremble in the
> presence of even an earthly prince? Who
> am I, that I should lift up mine eyes or raise
> my hands to the divine Majesty? The angels
> surround him. At his nod the earth trembles.
> And shall I, a miserable little pygmy, say 'I
> want this, I ask for that'? For I am dust and
> ashes and full of sin and I am speaking to the
> living, eternal and the true God."[3]

But these episodes are minor considerations in the
question of Luther's sanity. Our attention must move
to one of the most dramatic moments of Luther's life,
a dramatic moment for all of Christendom. The supreme trial of Luther's life, the occasion for his utmost

test, came at the Imperial Diet of Worms in the year 1521. Before the princes of the church and state, in the presence of the Holy Roman Emperor Charles, a coal miner's son was on trial for heresy.

Events had run out of control since the theological professor had tacked his Ninety-five Theses on the door of All Saints Church at Wittenburg. These were points of issue Luther was announcing for theological debate and dispute. He had no desire to flame them into a national or international fire. Some people, probably students, got hold of the theses and made use of the marvelous new invention of Gutenberg. Within two weeks the theses were the talk of Germany. Bainton borrows an expression from Karl Barth to explain what happened: "Luther was like a man climbing in the darkness a winding staircase in the steeple of an ancient cathedral. In the blackness he reached out to steady himself, and his hand laid hold of a rope. He was startled to hear the clanging of a bell."[4]

A whirlwind of controversy followed. The theses were forwarded to Rome, to Pope Leo. Legend has it that Leo read them and said, "Luther is a drunken German. He will feel different when he is sober." The fight was carried on between monastic orders and theologians. Luther engaged in debates, the most serious in Augsburg and Leipzig. Finally Luther was censured by the publication of a papal bull. Its title, *Exsurge Domine,* came from its opening words: "Arise, O Lord, and judge thy cause. A wild boar has invaded thy vineyard."

After the bull was published, Luther's books were

burned in Rome. He appealed for a hearing to the emperor. Finally the Diet met at Worms, where Luther was granted a safe conduct for travel to appear.

What happened at Worms was the stuff that legends are made of. In fact legends have arisen from the events. Hollywood has given its touch of glamour to the scene. The image of Luther that prevails is that of a valiant hero defying a wicked authority structure. Luther is asked, "Will you recant of your writings?"

We imagine Luther standing tall, unintimidated by the officials there, and saying with fist clenched in the air, "Here I stand!" Then we see him turn on his heel and walk boldly from the hall while the people cheer. He mounts his white horse and gallops off into the sunset to begin the Protestant Reformation.

That is not how it happened.

The first session met on April 17. The air was electric with excitement over the showdown. Luther had spoken boldly before his arrival, saying: "This shall be my recantation at Worms: 'Previously I said the pope is the vicar of Christ. I recant. Now I say the pope is the adversary of Christ and the apostle of the Devil.'"[5]

The crowd was expecting more bold statements. They held their breath, waiting for the wild boar to go on the rampage.

When the Imperial Diet opened, Luther stood in the center of the great hall. By his side was a table that contained his controversial books. An official asked Luther if the books were his. He replied in a voice that was barely a whisper: "The books are all mine, and I have written more." Then came the decisive question of Luther's readiness to recant. The assembly waited for his response. There was no raised fist, no defiant challenge. Again Luther answered almost inaudibly, "I beg you, give me time to think it over." As he had done at his first mass, Luther faltered. His confidence deserted him; the wild boar was suddenly like a whimpering pup. The emperor was shocked by the request and wondered if it might simply be a stalling tactic, a theological filibuster. Yet he granted clemency until the morrow, giving Luther twenty-four hours to think it over.

That night, in the solitude of his room, Luther wrote what I believe to be one of the most moving prayers ever written. His prayer reveals the soul of a humble man prostrate before his God, desperately seeking the courage to stand alone before hostile men. For Luther it was a private Gethsemane:

> O God, Almighty God everlasting! how dreadful is the world! behold how its mouth opens to swallow me up, and how small is my faith in thee! . . . Oh! the weakness of the flesh, and the power of Satan! If I am to depend upon any strength of this world—all is over. . . . The knell is struck. . . . Sentence is gone forth. . . . O God! O God! O thou, my God! help me against all the wisdom of this world. Do this, I beseech thee; thou shouldst do this . . . by thy own mighty power. . . . The work is not mine, but thine. I have no business here. . . . I have nothing to contend for with these great men of the world! I would gladly pass my

days in happiness and peace. But the cause is thine.... And it is righteous and everlasting! O Lord! help me! O faithful and unchangeable God! I lean not upon man. It were vain! Whatever is of man is tottering, whatever proceeds from him must fail. My God! my God! does thou not hear? My God! art thou no longer living? Nay, thou canst not die. Thou dost but hide thyself. Thou hast chosen me for this work. I know it! ... Therefore, O God, accomplish thine own will! Forsake me not, for the sake of thy well-beloved Son, Jesus Christ, my defense, my buckler, and my stronghold. Lord—where art thou? ... My God, where art thou? ... Come! I pray thee, I am ready.... Behold me prepared to lay down my life for thy truth ... suffering like a lamb. For the cause is holy. It is thine own! ... I will not let thee go! no, nor yet for all eternity! And though the world should be thronged with devils—and this body, which is the work of thine hands, should be cast forth, trodden under foot, cut in pieces, ... consumed to ashes, my soul is thine. Yes, I have thine own word to assure me of it. My soul belongs to thee, and will abide with thee forever! Amen! O God send help! ... Amen![6]

Late the next afternoon Luther returned to the hall. This time his voice did not quake or quiver. He tried to answer the question by giving a speech. His inquisitor finally demanded an answer: "I ask you,

Martin—answer candidly and without horns—do you or do you not repudiate your books and the errors which they contain?"[7]

Luther replied:

> Since then Your Majesty and your lordships desire a simple reply, I will answer without horns and without teeth. Unless I am convicted by Scripture and plain reason— I do not accept the authority of popes and councils, for they have contradicted each other—my conscience is captive to the Word of God. I cannot and I will not recant anything, for to go against conscience is neither right nor safe. Here I stand, I cannot do otherwise. God help me. Amen.[8]

The words of a crazy man? Perhaps. The question is raised how one man dare stand against pope and emperor, councils and creeds, against the entire organized authority of Christendom. What arrogance there must be to contradict the finest scholars and the highest officials of the church, to set his own powers of mind and biblical interpretation against that of the whole world. Is this egomania? Is it megalomania? Are these the musings of a biblical genius, a courageous saint, or the ravings of a maniac? Whatever the verdict, this lonely stand, for good or for evil, divided Christendom asunder.

As important as this event was to the church and to the personal history of Martin Luther, it was not the chief reason future scholars would judge Luther insane. There was something even more extraordinary, more morbid, indeed macabre about the man. It had to do with Luther's behavioral patterns while he was a monk in the monastery.

As a monk, Luther devoted himself to a rigorous kind of austerity. He set out to be the perfect monk. He fasted for days and indulged in severe forms of self-flagellation. He went beyond the rules of the monastery in matters of self-denial. His prayer vigils were longer than anyone else's. He refused the normal allotment of blankets and almost froze to death. He punished his body so severely that he later commented it was in the monk's cell that he did permanent damage to his digestive system. He wrote about his experience: "I was a good monk, and I kept the rule of my order so strictly that I may say that if ever a monk got to heaven by his monkery, it was I. All my brothers in the monastery who knew me will bear me out. If I had kept on any longer, I should have killed myself with vigils, prayers, reading, and other work."[9]

The most bizarre of Luther's practices involved his habit of daily confession. The requirement was that all one's sins be confessed. Luther could not go a day without sinning, so he felt it necessary to go to the confessional every day, seeking absolution.

Confession was a regular part of the monastic life. The other brothers came regularly to their confessors and said, "Father, I have sinned. Last night I stayed up after 'lights out' and read my Bible with a candle." Or, "Yesterday at lunchtime I coveted Brother Philip's potato salad." (How much trouble can a monk get into in a monastery?) The Father Confessor would hear the confession, grant priestly absolution, and assign a small penance to be performed. That was it. The whole transaction took only a few minutes.

Not so with Brother Martin. He was driving his Father Confessor to distraction. Luther was not satisfied with a brief recitation of his sins. He wanted to make sure that no sin in his life was left unconfessed. He entered the confessional and stayed for hours every day. On one occasion Luther spent six hours confessing the sins he had committed in the previous day!

The superiors of the monastery began to wonder about Luther. They considered the possibility that he was a "goldbricker," preferring to spend his waking hours in the confessional rather than to study and perform his other tasks. Concern arose that perhaps he was mentally unbalanced, rapidly moving to serious psychosis. His mentor, Staupitz, finally grew angry and scolded Luther: "'Look here,' he said, 'if you expect Christ to forgive you, come in with something to forgive—parricide, blasphemy, adultery—instead of all these peccadilloes. . . . Man, God is not angry with you. You are angry with God. Don't you know that God commands you to hope?'"[10]

Here it is! Here is the aspect of Luther that has most brought the verdict of insanity. The man was radically abnormal. His guilt complex was unlike anyone's before him. He was so morbid in his guilt, so disturbed in his emotions, that he could no longer function as a normal human being. He could not even function as a normal monk. He was still running from the lightning bolt. Bainton sums up his condition:

In consequence the most frightful insecurity beset him. Panic invaded his spirit. The conscience became so disquieted as to start and tremble at the stirring of a wind-blown leaf. The horror of nightmare gripped the soul, the dread of one waking in the dusk to look into the eyes of him who has come to take his life. The heavenly champions all withdrew; the fiend beckoned with leering summons to the impotent soul. These were the torments which Luther repeatedly testified were far worse than any physical ailment that he had ever endured.

His description tallies so well with a recognized type of mental malady that again one is tempted to wonder whether his disturbance should be regarded as arising from authentic religious difficulties or from gastric or glandular deficiencies.[11]

What accounts for Luther's behavior? One thing is certain: Whatever defense mechanisms normal people have to mute the accusing voice of conscience, Luther was lacking.

Some theorists argue that people may have a more accurate view of reality when they are insane than when they are sane. We think of the anxiety-stricken man who goes to the psychiatrist and complains that he is so paralyzed by fear that he cannot attend a church picnic. When the psychiatrist probes, the man explains that he could be involved in a car crash on the way to the picnic, be struck by a poisonous snake while at the picnic, be hit by lightning if a storm comes up, or choke to death on a hot dog.

All of these fears represent sober possibilities. Life is dangerous business. Nowhere are we safe from a multitude of life-threatening dangers. Howard Hughes, with all his millions, could not find an environment where he was totally safe from the attack of hostile germs. The psychiatrist cannot prove that all picnics are safe. The man's perception of all the things that could go wrong is accurate, but he is still abnormal because he has lost the defenses that enable us to ignore the clear and present dangers that surround us every day.

One aspect of Luther's background and personality is often overlooked by the psychological analysts. They miss the point that before Luther went to the monastery, he had already distinguished himself as one of the brightest young minds in Europe in the field of jurisprudence. Luther was brilliant. There was nothing wrong with his brain. His grasp of subtle and difficult points of the law made him a standout. Some heralded him as a legal genius.

It has been said many times that there is a fine line between genius and insanity and that some people move back and forth across it. Perhaps that was the problem Luther had.

He was not crazy. He was a genius. He had a superior understanding of law. Once he applied his astute legal mind to the law of God, he saw things that many people miss.

Luther examined the Great Commandment, " 'Love the Lord your God with all your heart and with all your soul and with all your strength and with all your mind'; and, 'Love your neighbor as yourself'" (Luke 10:27). Then he asked himself, "What is the Great Transgression?" Some answer this question by saying that the great sin is murder, adultery, blasphemy, or unbelief. Luther disagreed. He concluded that if the Great Commandment was to love God with all the heart, then the Great Transgression was to fail to love God with all the heart. He saw a balance between great obligations and great sins.

Most people do not think that way. None of us keeps the Great Commandment for five minutes. We may think that we do in a surface way, but on a moment's reflection it is clear that we don't love God with our whole heart or our whole mind or our whole strength. We don't love our neighbor as we love ourselves. We may do everything in our power to avoid thinking about this at a deep level, but there is always that nagging sense in the back of our minds to accuse us of the certain knowledge that, in fact, we violate the Great Commandment every day. Like Isaiah, we also know that no one else keeps the Great Commandment either. Herein is our comfort: Nobody is perfect. We all fall short of perfect love for God, so why worry about it? It doesn't drive sane people to the confessional for six hours a day. If God punished everyone who failed to keep the Great Commandment, He would have to punish everyone in the world. The test is too great, too demanding; it is not fair. God will have to judge us all on a curve.

Luther didn't see it that way. He realized that if God graded on a curve, He would have to compromise His own holiness. To count on God doing so is supreme arrogance and supreme foolishness as well. God does not lower His own standards to accommodate us. He remains altogether holy, altogether righteous, and altogether just. But we are unjust, and therein lies our dilemma. Luther's legal mind was haunted by the question, How can an unjust person survive in the presence of a just God? Where everyone else was at ease in the matter, Luther was in agony: "Do you not know that God dwells in light inaccessible? We weak and ignorant creatures want to probe and understand the incomprehensible majesty of the unfathomable light of the wonder of God. We approach; we prepare ourselves to approach. What wonder then that his majesty overpowers us and shatters!"[12]

Luther was the polar opposite to the biblical character of the rich young ruler who came to Jesus inquiring about his salvation: "A certain ruler asked him, 'Good teacher, what must I do to inherit eternal life?' 'Why do you call me good?' Jesus answered. 'No one is good—except God alone. You know the commandments: "Do not commit adultery, do not murder, do not steal, do not give false testimony, honor your father and mother"'" (Luke 18:18-20).

People often miss something in this well-known meeting between Jesus and the rich ruler. It is the significance of the man's greeting to Jesus. He called Him "Good teacher."

Jesus did not miss the significance of it. Jesus knew at once that He was talking to a man who had a superficial understanding of the meaning of the word *good*. The man wanted to talk to Jesus about salvation.

Instead, Jesus subtly turned the conversation around to a discussion about what goodness was. He took the opportunity to give the man an unforgettable lesson on the meaning of "good."

Jesus focused on the man's greeting: "Why do you call me good?" He accented the question with a further qualification: "No one is good—except God alone." Let a red alert sound here. Some people, even learned theologians, have stumbled over Jesus' comments. Some hear Jesus saying in effect, "Why are you calling me good? I am not good. Only God is good. I am not God. I am not good."

By no means was Jesus denying His own deity here. And He was not denying His own goodness. Given the right understanding, it would have been perfectly fitting for the rich ruler to call Jesus good. Jesus was good. He was the incarnation of the good. The point is, however, that the rich man was not aware of that. He was honoring Jesus as a great teacher, but that is all he saw in Him. He had no idea he was speaking to God Incarnate.

The rich young ruler obviously did not know his Bible. He had failed to understand the meaning of Psalm 14: "The fool says in his heart, 'There is no God.' They are corrupt, their deeds are vile; there is no one who does good. The LORD looks down from heaven on the sons of men to see if there are any who understand, any who seek God. All have turned aside, they have together become corrupt; there is no one who does good, not even one" (Ps. 14:1-3).

This psalm is quoted and amplified in the New Testament by the apostle Paul. The message is unmistakable. No one does good, not even one. The "not even one" erases all possibility for misunderstanding. The indictment allows for no exceptions save for the Son of God, who alone achieves goodness.

The human spirit recoils from such a universal indictment. Surely the Scriptures exaggerate. We know several people who do good. We see people perform good deeds frequently. We grant that no one is perfect. We all slip up from time to time. But we do perform a few good deeds now and then, don't we? No! This is precisely the way the rich young ruler was thinking. He was measuring goodness by the wrong standard. He was evaluating good deeds from an outward vantage point.

God commands that we do certain good things. He commands us to give to the poor. We give to the poor. That is a good deed, isn't it? Yes and no. It is good in the sense that our outward act conforms to what God commands. In that sense we do good often. But God also looks at the heart. He is concerned about our deepest motivations. For a good deed to pass the standard of God's goodness, it must flow out of a heart that loves God perfectly and loves our neighbor perfectly as well. Since none of us achieves that perfect love for God and our neighbor, all of our outwardly good deeds are tarnished. They carry the blemish of the imperfections of our inner motivations. The logic of the Bible is this: Since no one has a perfect heart, no one does a perfect deed.

The law of God is the mirror of true righteousness. When we set our works before this mirror, the reflection in it tells us of our imperfections. Jesus held this mirror up before the eyes of the rich young ruler: "You know the commandments: 'Do not commit adultery, do not murder, do not steal. . . .'" (Luke 18:20). It is important to note here that the commandments Jesus listed for the young ruler were those included in the so-called second table of the law, the commandments that deal with our responsibilities toward fellow human beings. These are the commandments that concern adultery, murder, stealing, and so on. Noticeably absent in Jesus' summary were the first few commandments that deal explicitly with our direct obligations to God.

How did the rich man answer? He was not bothered. He looked calmly in the mirror and saw no imperfections. He replied: "All these I have kept since I was a boy" (Luke 18:21).

Imagine the arrogance or the ignorance of the man. I find it difficult to understand Jesus' patience. I could not have contained myself. I would have instantly expressed my indignation by saying something like, "What! You have kept the Ten Commandments since you were a boy! You haven't kept any of the Ten Commandments for the last five minutes. Didn't you hear the Sermon on the Mount? Don't you realize that if you are unjustly angry with someone, you have violated the deeper meaning of the law against murder? Don't you know that if you lust after a woman, you break the deeper law of adultery? Don't you ever covet? Do you always honor your parents? You are mad or blind. Your obedience has been superficial at best. You obey only on the surface."

That is how I would have handled it. But it is not the way Jesus handled it. Jesus was more subtle, and more effective: "When Jesus heard this, he said to him, 'You still lack one thing. Sell everything you have and give to the poor, and you will have treasure in heaven. Then come, follow me'" (Luke 18:22).

If ever Jesus spoke with tongue in cheek, it was here. If we take Jesus' words literally, we would be forced to conclude that the conversation took place between the two most righteous men in history, that it was a dialogue between the Lamb without blemish and a lamb with only one blemish. I would be delighted to hear from Jesus that my moral perfection lacked only one thing.

We know better. If we speculate and try to get into the secret recesses of Jesus' mind, we can imagine a thought process that went something like this: *Oh, you have kept all the commandments since you were a child. Well, let's see. What is the first commandment? Oh, yes, "You shall have no other gods before me." Let's see how you do with that one.*

Jesus put him to the test. If anything in the rich man's life came before God, it was his money. Jesus set the challenge precisely at this point, at the point of the man's obedience to commandment number one: "Go, sell all that you have...."

What did the man do? How did he handle his only blemish? He walked away sorrowfully, for he had great possessions. The man was put to the test of the Ten Commandments, and he flunked out after the first question.

The point of this narrative is not to lay down a law

that a Christian must get rid of all private property. The point is for us to understand what obedience is and what goodness actually requires. Jesus called the man's bluff, and the man folded.

When Jesus met another young man centuries later, He did not have to go through an elaborate object lesson to help the man understand his sin. He never said to Luther, "*One* thing you lack." Luther already knew that he lacked a multitude of things. He was a lawyer; he had studied the Old Testament Law; he knew the demands of a pure and holy God, and it was driving him crazy.

The genius of Luther ran up against a legal dilemma that he could not solve. There seemed to be no solution possible. The question that nagged him day and night was how a just God could accept an unjust man. He knew that his eternal destiny rode on the answer. But he could not find the answer. Lesser minds went merrily along their way, enjoying the bliss of ignorance. They were satisfied to think that God would compromise His own excellence and let them into heaven. After all, heaven would not be the marvelous place it was cracked up to be if they were excluded from it. God must grade on a curve. Boys will be boys, and God is big enough not to get all excited about a few moral blemishes.

Two things separated Luther from the rest of men: First, he knew who God was. Second, he understood the demands of God's law. He had mastered the law. Unless he came to understand the gospel, he would die in torment.

Then it happened: Luther's ultimate religious experience. There were no lightning bolts, no flying inkwells. It took place in quietness, in the solitude of his study. Luther's so-called "tower experience" changed the course of world history. It was an experience that involved a new understanding of God, a new understanding of His divine justice. It was an understanding of how God can be merciful without compromising His justice. It was a new understanding of how a holy God expresses a holy love:

> I greatly longed to understand Paul's Epistle to the Romans and nothing stood in the way but that one expression, "the justice of God," because I took it to mean that justice whereby God is just and deals justly in punishing the unjust. My situation was that, although an impeccable monk, I stood before God as a sinner troubled in conscience, and I had no confidence that my merit would assuage him. Therefore I did not love a just and angry God, but rather hated and murmured against him. Yet I clung to the dear Paul and had a great yearning to know what he meant.
>
> Night and day I pondered until I saw the connection between the justice of God and the statement that "the just shall live by faith." Then I grasped that the justice of God is that righteousness by which through grace and sheer mercy God justifies us through faith. Thereupon I felt myself to be reborn and to

have gone through open doors into paradise. The whole of Scripture took on a new meaning, and whereas before the "justice of God" had filled me with hate, now it became to me inexpressibly sweet in greater love. This passage of Paul became to me a gate of heaven....

If you have a true faith that Christ is your Saviour, then at once you have a gracious God, for faith leads you in and opens up God's heart and will, that you should see pure grace and overflowing love. This it is to behold God in faith that you should look upon his fatherly, friendly heart, in which there is no anger nor ungraciousness. He who sees God as angry does not see him rightly but looks only on a curtain as if a dark cloud had been drawn across his face.[13]

Like Isaiah before him, Luther felt the burning coal on his lips. He knew what it meant to be undone. He was shattered by the mirror of a holy God. He said later that before he could get a taste of heaven, God had to dangle him first over the pit of hell. God did not drop His servant into the pit; He saved his life from the pit. He proved that He was a God who was both just and the justifier. When Luther understood the gospel for the first time, the doors of paradise swung open, and he walked through.

"The just shall live by faith." This was the battle cry of the Protestant Reformation. The idea that justification is by faith alone, by the merits of Christ alone, was so central to the gospel that Luther called it "the article upon which the church stands or falls." Luther knew that it was the article by which he would stand or fall.

Once Luther grasped Paul's teaching in Romans, he was reborn. The burden of his guilt was lifted. The crazed torment was ended. This meant so much to the man that he was able to stand against pope and council, prince and emperor, and, if necessary, the whole world. He had walked through the gates of paradise, and no one was going to drag him back. Luther was a Protestant who knew what he was protesting.

Was Luther crazy? Perhaps. But if he was, our prayer is that God would send to this earth an epidemic of such insanity that we too may taste of the righteousness that is by faith alone.

Allowing God's Holiness to Touch Our Lives

As you reflect about what you have learned and rediscovered about God's holiness, answer these questions. Use a journal to record your responses to God's holiness, or discuss your responses with a friend.

1. When you look into the mirror of God's holiness, what do you see? What do you learn about yourself and about God?
2. What do you do with your guilt about your sin?
3. What does "the just shall live by faith" mean to you personally?
4. How can you worship God for justifying you?

Holy Justice

Justice is regarded as the highest
of all virtues, more admirable than
morning star and evening star.

ARISTOTLE

Martin Luther understood how serious the problem is for unjust people to live in the presence of a just and holy God. Just as Luther was a monk of monks, so Paul was a Pharisee of Pharisees. Both were brilliant men, highly educated. It was said of Paul that he was the most educated man in Palestine at the time of his conversion. He had the equivalent of two Ph.D.'s by the time he was twenty-one years old. He also struggled deeply with the law and the question of the justice of God. Luther the monk and Paul the Pharisee both were consumed by the problem of holy justice. They were both students of the Old Testament Law before they became advocates of the gospel.

Whoever reads the Old Testament must struggle with the apparent brutality of God's judgment found there. For many people this is as far as they read. They stumble over the violent passages we call the "hard sayings." Some people see these sayings as sufficient reason to reject Christianity out of hand. These hard sayings seem ample reason to hold the Old Testament God in contempt. Others try to soften the blow by turning the Old Testament into a religious parable or by applying a method of cut and paste, assigning the more brutal passages to the level of primitive myth. Some even go so far as to argue that the Old Testament God is a different God from the New Testament God—a shadowy God with a bad temper, a kind of demonic deity whose blazing wrath is beneath the dignity of the New Testament God of love.

In this chapter I want to stare the Old Testament God right in the eye. I want to look at the most difficult, most offensive passages we can find in the Old Testament and see if we can make any sense of them. We will look at the swift and sudden judgment that falls on Nadab and Abihu, the sons of Aaron; we will look at God's striking Uzzah dead for touching the ark of the covenant; we will look at the lengthy list of crimes for which God commanded capital punishment; we will look at the slaughter of women and children allegedly done under the orders of God. Be warned. This chapter is not for the weak of stomach or of heart. We will stare into the abyss of the Most Terrible, if you are willing to read along.

Let's look first at Nadab and Abihu. These two men were priests, sons of Aaron, the high priest. God had personally selected Aaron to be the first high priest. Together with Moses, Aaron had led the people of Israel through the wilderness. "Aaron's sons Nadab and Abihu took their censers, put fire in them and added incense; and they offered unauthorized fire before the LORD, contrary to his command. So fire came out from the presence of the LORD and consumed them, and they died before the LORD" (Lev. 10:1-2). If any people in Israel had a close relationship with God, it was Moses and Aaron. One might expect a little leeway from God in dealing with Aaron's sons. But there was none. For one transgression at the altar, God reacted swiftly and violently, wiping them out on the spot. It was not as if they profaned the altar with prostitutes or offered human sacrifices as did the Molech cult. All Nadab and Abihu did was offer some "strange fire" there. We are not sure exactly what the strange fire was. It sounds as if the situation was merely a question of young priests doing some creative experimenting with the liturgy. A censurable offense, perhaps. But the death penalty? Without the benefit of a trial? Immediate, summary execution?

Throughout the years people have tried to offer a natural explanation for what happened to Nadab and Abihu. Immanuel Velikovsky, scientist friend of Albert Einstein's, was one of those people.

Velikovsky shocked the geological world with his theories that changes in the earth's surface were made suddenly by a catastrophic upheaval caused by a planet or giant comet that came so close to the earth that it reversed the magnetic poles and forced the earth to start spinning in the opposite direction. Imagine a top spinning as fast as it can. Then, instantly, it is made to spin in the opposite direction. If there were water inside the top, what would happen to it? It would become a tidal wave in the opposite direction. Part of Velikovsky's theory suggests that a meteoric shower bombarded the earth that included within its content great volumes of petroleum, filling the fissures on the earth's surface and causing great deposits of oil to form under the earth. (Consider the oil-rich region of the Middle East.)

This theory suggests that Nadab and Abihu found some oil lying around, and they wondered what it was. They decided to see how it worked if it was mixed with the burning substances at the altar. When they put it in the fire, *whoosh*, it ignited and exploded, killing the priests instantly. In a primitive society this would be viewed as a sudden act of judgment by the gods. In Velikovsky's view, the deaths of Nadab and Abihu were accidents, a tragic case of children playing with unknown fire.

The Bible views the story differently. The Bible records the event as a supernatural judgment of God. It may have been enacted through natural means, but it is clear that the death of Nadab and Abihu was no accident. It must be ascribed to the wrath and judgment of God.

How did Aaron view the event? I suppose he was angry and hurt. It was a calamity for Aaron and his remaining family. He had dedicated his entire life to the service of God. His sons were following in his footsteps. He could remember the day of their consecration and the pride he felt when they were set apart for the priesthood. It was a family matter. What thanks did he get from the God he served? God summarily executed his sons for what appeared to be a minor infraction of the rules of the altar.

Aaron rushed to see Moses and tell him about it. It was as if Aaron were saying, "Okay, God, I'm going to tell on you. I'm going straight to Moses. You're going to have to deal with us both on this one." So Aaron went to Moses and pled his case: "Moses then said to Aaron, 'This is what the LORD spoke of when he said: "Among those who approach me I will show myself holy; in the sight of all the people I will be honored"'" (Lev. 10:3).

Moses gave Aaron the answer of the Lord. He reminded him of the original consecration of the priests. They had been set apart for a sacred task and solemnly charged with the precise requirements of their office. They had the privilege of ministering before a holy God. Each vessel in the tabernacle was made to precise specifications, and each item was sanctified by elaborate measures commanded by God. There was no ambiguity to be found in these commands. With respect to the altar of incense, Aaron and his sons were specifically instructed in the proper procedures. God had spoken: "Do not offer on this altar any other incense or any burnt offering or grain offering, and do not pour a drink offering on it. Once a year Aaron shall make atonement on its horns. This annual atonement must be made with the blood of the atoning sin offering for the generations to come. It is most holy to the LORD" (Exod. 30:9-10).

The instructions had been clear. The altar of incense was declared by God to be "most holy." When Nadab and Abihu offered strange or unauthorized fire on it, they were acting in clear defiance of God. Theirs was an act of blatant rebellion, an inexcusable profaning of the Holy Place. They committed a sin of arrogance, an act of treason against God: They profaned a most holy place.

God's judgment was swift. His explanation to Moses was clear: "I will show myself holy; in the sight of all the people I will be honored." These were not words of future prophecy or prediction. When God said, "I will," He meant it as a divine command, a command no one dare countermand.

The capstone of this episode is found in the last sentence of Leviticus 10:3: "Aaron remained silent."

What else could Aaron do? The debate was over. The evidence was in, and God had rendered His verdict. The sons of Aaron had been explicitly forbidden from offering such fire. They committed an act of disobedience, and God had lowered the gavel of His justice on them. So Aaron was silent. He held his peace. He could think of no excuse to offer, no protest to make. Like sinners at the Last Judgment, his mouth was stopped.

Here is an example of God's punitive justice, the justice by which He punishes the guilty. Is this punishment cruel and unusual? Does it in fact go beyond the limits of justice and cross the border into injustice?

Built into our concept of justice is the idea that the punishment must fit the crime. If the punishment is more severe than the crime, then an injustice has been committed. The Bible makes it clear that Nadab and Abihu could not plead ignorance as an excuse for their sin. God had made His instructions clear to them. They knew that they were not allowed to offer unauthorized fire on the altar. That they sinned is easy for us to see. But they never dreamed their sin was so serious that it would prompt God to execute them on the spot. Here we meet an example that screams of harshness from the hand of God, of a punishment that is far too cruel and unusual for the crime. Such a measure of punishment not only puzzles us, it staggers us.

How do we square this narrative with what Genesis teaches earlier about the character of God's justice? Genesis asserts that the judge of all the earth *will do right* (Gen. 18:25). The basic assumption of Israel is that God's judgments are always according to righteousness. His justice is never unfair, never whimsical, never tyrannical. It is impossible for God to be unjust, because His justice is holy.

If we struggle with the story of Nadab and Abihu, we meet even greater difficulty with the story of Uzzah. When David ascended to the kingship of Israel, he moved quickly to consolidate his kingdom. He conferred with his officers and military commanders and decided to bring the ark of the covenant, Israel's most sacred vessel, out of "retirement" and back to a central place. The ark had been captured by the Philistines; and it was said that in that fateful day, the glory had departed from Israel. When the sacred ark was captured, Israel's greatest treasure was stolen and carried off to the pagan temple of Dagon. When the ark was returned, it was placed in safekeeping awaiting the appropriate time for its public restoration to a position of prominence in the midst of the nation. Finally, the hour came, and David wanted the glory back. He said: " 'Let us bring the ark of our God back to us, for we did not inquire of it during the reign of Saul.' The whole assembly agreed to do this, because it seemed right to all the people" (1 Chron. 13:3-4).

The ark was the rallying point for the nation. It was the throne of God, the sacred seat of the Most High.

It had been constructed and ornamented by the strict design of God Himself. It was to be housed in the *Sanctus Sanctorum,* the Holy of Holies. The ark was a chest made of acacia wood, overlaid with gold on the inside and outside. It had a gold molding around it. Four gold rings were fastened to its feet so that poles could be inserted through the rings to carry the chest. The poles were also made of acacia wood and overlaid with gold.

The lid of the chest was called an "atonement cover." It was also made of pure gold. Two cherubim made of hammered gold were mounted on each end of the chest, facing each other with their wings spread upward. This was the sacred object that David ordered returned to Jerusalem.

> They moved the ark of God from Abinadab's house on a new cart, with Uzzah and Ahio guiding it. David and all the Israelites were celebrating with all their might before God, with songs and with harps, lyres, tambourines, cymbals and trumpets.
>
> When they came to the threshing floor of Kidon, Uzzah reached out his hand to steady the ark, because the oxen stumbled. The LORD's anger burned against Uzzah, and he struck him down because he had put his hand on the ark. So he died there before God.
>
> Then David was angry because the LORD's wrath had broken out against Uzzah.
> (1 Chron. 13:7-11)

If God made David angry with this violent outburst of wrath, how much more unsettled does it make a reader who is unskilled in theology? David was a man after God's own heart. Not only was he a masterful king, an accomplished musician, and a champion warrior, but he was also a premier theologian.

Even more than the case of Nadab and Abihu, the execution of Uzzah stirs protests from readers who have been taught that God is a God of love and kindness. The Bible says of God that He is long-suffering and slow to anger. It sure didn't take His anger long to reach the boiling point with Uzzah. Uzzah touched the ark, and *wham!* God exploded in fury.

Again, efforts have been made to soften the harshness of this account by seeking a natural explanation for Uzzah's death. It has been suggested that Uzzah had so much respect for the sacred ark that when he touched it, he was so overcome with fright that he had a heart attack and died on the spot. He was plain scared to death. This explanation absolves God of any responsibility in the matter. The biblical writer's interpretation is merely an example of primitive superstition sprinkled throughout the Old Testament.

People reach for such explanations not only because our culture has an incurable allergy to all things supernatural but also because the story so offends our sense of justice. Look again at what happened. The ark was being transported by oxcart toward Jerusalem. It was a joyous day of national celebration. The glory was returning to the Holy City. The roads were crowded with people. The gala parade was punctuated by the sounds of the harps, lyres, tambourines, cymbals, and trumpets.

Imagine the spectacle: It was like a parade with seventy-six trombones. People danced in the streets.

The oxen suddenly stumbled, and the cart tottered precariously. The chest slid from its mooring and was in danger of falling into the dirt and being sullied by the mud. It was unthinkable that this precious object be desecrated by falling in the dirt.

Surely Uzzah's reaction was instinctive. He did what any pious Jew would do to keep the ark from falling into the mud. He reached out his hand to steady the ark, to protect the holy object from falling. It was not a premeditated act of defiance toward God. It was a reflex action. From our vantage point it seems like an act of heroism. We think that Uzzah should have heard the voice of God shouting down from heaven, crying, "Thank you, Uzzah!"

God didn't do that.

Instead, He killed Uzzah. He slaughtered him on the spot. Another summary execution.

What was Uzzah's sin? To answer that, we must look back in Jewish history to the formation of the priesthood and the special commands that God had given them. To be a priest in Israel, one had to be from the tribe of Levi. All priests were Levites, but not all Levites were priests. A special family branch of the Levites were the clan of Kohathites. As the name indicates, these were the descendants of Kohath. The Kohathites were consecrated by God to a highly specialized task. They were trained for one basic job—to take care of the sacred articles of the tabernacle: "This is the work of the Kohathites in the Tent of Meeting: the care of the most holy things" (Num. 4:4).

It is important to remember that the tabernacle was a tent. It was portable. When the tribes of Israel moved, they carried the tabernacle with them so that God would be in their midst. When the tabernacle was transported, it was necessary first to cover and shield the holy vessels. We read, "After Aaron and his sons have finished covering the holy furnishings and all the holy articles, and when the camp is ready to move, the Kohathites are to come to do the carrying. *But they must not touch the holy things or they will die.* The Kohathites are to carry those things that are in the Tent of Meeting" (Num. 4:15, italics added).

To reinforce this command, God adds further provisions and stipulations:

> The LORD said to Moses and Aaron, "See that the Kohathite tribal clans are not cut off from the Levites. So that they may live and not die when they come near the most holy things, do this for them: Aaron and his sons are to go into the sanctuary and assign to each man his work and what he is to carry. But the Kohathites must not go in to look at the holy things, even for a moment, or they will die." (Num. 4:17-20)

Uzzah was probably a Kohathite. He knew exactly what his duties were. He had been trained thoroughly in the discipline of his calling. He understood that God had declared that the touching of the ark of the covenant was a capital offense. No Kohathite, under any circumstance, was ever permitted to touch the ark. No emergency was grounds for breaking that inviolate command. The elaborate construction of the ark, complete with golden rings through which long poles were inserted, was so fashioned as to make it clear that the ark itself was not to be touched. The men commissioned to transport the ark could touch only the poles and the rings. Then it was the task of the Kohathites to carry the ark by these long poles. No provision was made for hurrying the procedure by transporting the ark via an oxcart.

We must ask the question, What was the ark doing on an oxcart in the first place? God was so strict about the holy things of the tabernacle that the Kohathites were not allowed even to gaze upon the ark. This, too, was a capital crime. God had decreed that if a Kohathite merely glanced at the ark in the Holy of Holies for an instant, he would die. Not only was Uzzah forbidden to touch the ark, he was forbidden even to look at it.

He touched it anyway. He stretched out his hand and placed it squarely on the ark, steadying it in place lest it fall to the ground. An act of holy heroism? No! It was an act of arrogance, a sin of presumption. Uzzah assumed that his hand was less polluted than the earth. But it wasn't the ground or the mud that would desecrate the ark; it was the touch of man. The earth is an obedient creature. It does what God tells it to do. It brings forth its yield in its season. It obeys the laws of nature that God has established. When the temperature falls to a certain point, the ground freezes. When water is added to the dust, it becomes mud, just as God designed it. The ground doesn't commit cosmic treason. There is nothing polluted about the ground.

God did not want His holy throne touched by that which was contaminated by evil, that which was in rebellion to Him, that which by its ungodly revolt had brought the whole creation to ruin and caused the ground and the sky and the waters of the sea to groan together in travail, waiting for the day of redemption. Man. It was man's touch that was forbidden.

Uzzah was not an innocent man. He was not punished without a warning. He was not punished without violating a law. There was no caprice in this act of divine judgment. There was nothing arbitrary or whimsical about what God did in that moment. But there was something unusual about it. The execution's suddenness and finality take us by surprise and at once shock and offend us.

There is a reason why we are offended, indeed angered, by the story of Uzzah and the story of Nadab and Abihu. We find these things difficult to stomach because we do not understand four vitally important biblical concepts: *holiness, justice, sin,* and *grace.* We do not understand what it means to be holy. We do not understand what justice is. We do not understand what sin is. We do not understand what grace is.

The story of Uzzah is an example of divine justice. It is not an example of divine mercy. But we cannot begin to understand divine mercy until we first have some understanding of divine justice.

When the Bible speaks of God's justice, it usually links it to divine righteousness. God's justice is *according to righteousness.* There is no such thing as justice according to unrighteousness. There is no such thing as evil justice in God. The justice of God is always and ever an expression of His holy character.

The word *justice* in the Bible refers to a conformity to a rule or a norm. God plays by the rules. The ultimate norm of justice is His own holy character. His righteousness is of two sorts. We distinguish God's internal righteousness from His external righteousness. What God *does* is always consistent with who God *is.* He always acts according to His holy character. God's internal righteousness is the moral excellence of His character. It is rooted in His absolute purity. There is no "shadow of turning" in Him. As a holy God, He is utterly incapable of an unholy act. Only unholy beings commit unjust and unrighteous acts.

There is a consistency in God, a "straightness" about Him. Human unrighteousness is often described in terms of our being not straight. We are crooked. It is not by accident that we often refer to criminals as "crooks." Crooks are so called because they are crooked; they are not straight. God is straight. His straightness is seen in His outward behavior, His external righteousness. In all eternity God has never done a crooked thing. He killed Nadab and Abihu. He killed Uzzah. He did the same thing to Ananias and Sapphira in the New Testament. These were righteous acts of judgment.

The Bible clearly teaches that God is the Supreme Judge of the universe. The question we ask after reading about Uzzah is this: Is God qualified for the job?

To function as the Supreme Judge of heaven and earth, He ought to be just. If the Supreme Judge is unjust, we have no hope of justice ever prevailing. We know that earthly judges can be corrupt. They take bribes; they show partiality; at times they act from ignorance. They make mistakes.

Not so with God. There is no corruption in Him. No one can bribe Him. He refuses to show partiality. He shows no favoritism (Acts 10:34). He never acts out of ignorance. He does not make mistakes. Bumper stickers in this world may demand, "Impeach Nixon," but only a fool asks for the impeachment of God.

The patriarch Abraham wrestled with the question of the justice of God. God announced that He was going to destroy Sodom and Gomorrah. He planned to annihilate the cities totally—men, women, and children. Abraham was disturbed by this, concerned that in the visitation of divine wrath on the cities, the innocent would perish along with the guilty. If God wiped out the cities in an act of judgment, Abraham feared that the judgment would be indiscriminate, like a teacher punishing a whole class for the sins of one student:

> Then Abraham approached him and said: "Will you sweep away the righteous with the wicked? What if there are fifty righteous people in the city? Will you really sweep it away and not spare the place for the sake of the fifty righteous people in it? Far be it from you to do such a thing—to kill the righteous with the wicked, treating the righteous and

the wicked alike. Far be it from you! Will
not the Judge of all the earth do right?"
(Gen. 18:23-25)

"Will not the Judge of all the earth do right?" A
more rhetorical question has never been asked. Abraham assumed that to kill the righteous along with the
wicked was far removed from any possibility with
God. "Far be it from you!" Abraham had no idea how
far such an act would be from God. There was never
a remote possibility that God would kill innocent
people along with the guilty. For God to do that, He
would have to cease being holy. He would have to
stop being God.

God was willing to bend over backward for
Abraham. He said He would spare the whole city
if Abraham could find forty-five righteous people
in it. He would spare it for the sake of thirty, for the
sake of ten. Abraham's task was made more simple
by 80 percent. All he had to do was to find ten righteous people, and God would spare the whole city.
The implication of the text is that God would have
spared it for *one* person if Abraham could find one.
What happened to Sodom and Gomorrah? "Early
the next morning Abraham got up and returned to
the place where he had stood before the LORD. He
looked down toward Sodom and Gomorrah, toward
all the land of the plain, and he saw dense smoke
rising from the land, like smoke from a furnace"
(Gen. 19:27-28).

The Judge of heaven and earth did right. No innocent people were punished. God's justice is never di-

vorced from His righteousness. He never condemns the innocent. He never clears the guilty. He never punishes with undue severity. He never fails to reward righteousness. His justice is perfect justice.

God does not always act with justice. Sometimes He acts with mercy. Mercy is not justice, but it also is not injustice. Injustice violates righteousness. Mercy manifests kindness and grace and does no violence to righteousness. We may see *nonjustice* in God, which is *mercy,* but we never see *injustice* in God.

Again we ask, What about the obvious difference between the tone of the New Testament and that of the Old Testament? The Old Testament seems to show God as being more harsh than the New Testament does. Consider the matter of capital punishment in the Old Testament. The Old Testament lists numerous crimes that are punishable by death, including the following:

striking or cursing
   parents
desecrating sacrificial
   offerings
murder
kidnapping
idolatry
child sacrifice
blasphemy
Sabbath violations
the practice of magic
consulting mediums
   and wizards

unlawful divorce
homosexual practices
incest
bestiality
prostitution of virgins
rape
practicing false
   prophecy
refusing to obey the
   verdict of a priest-
   judge
bearing false witness in
   a capital case

This is a partial list of Old Testament crimes that called for the death penalty. Against the tone of the New Testament the list seems harsh.

A few years ago *Time* magazine reported an incident that took place in the state of Maryland. A truck driver was arrested for drunk and disorderly conduct. When the police officers arrived on the scene to arrest the man, he became abusive. He used filthy language in a boisterous manner, calling the officers every name he could think of. The police were infuriated by his verbal abuse. When the man was brought before the magistrate, he was still being abusive. The maximum penalty the magistrate could impose for drunk and disorderly conduct was a one-hundred-dollar fine and thirty days in jail.

The magistrate became so angry that he wanted to "throw the book" at him. He found an antiquated law still on the books in Maryland; it was in disuse but had never been repealed. The statute prohibited public blasphemy.

Since the man had publicly profaned and blasphemed the name of God as part of the verbal abuse he hurled at the police, the magistrate tacked on another one-hundred-dollar fine and an additional thirty days in jail.

The *Time* news editor reported this incident in a spirit of moral outrage. His complaint was not that penalties for blasphemy involved a violation of the separation of church and state. His outrage was based on his charge that to put a man in jail for sixty days and to fine him two hundred dollars was a gross miscarriage of justice. Such a penalty was too severe. It was cruel and unusual.

Evidently the news editor was not upset about the penalties imposed for drunk and disorderly conduct. It was the punishment for blasphemy that he could not handle. This is in strong contrast to the law code God established in Israel. The truck driver could rejoice that he wasn't arrested by Aaron. In the Old Testament the best lawyer in Israel could not get his client a one-hundred-dollar fine for public blasphemy. The question we face is, What is worse, creating a public disturbance by getting drunk, or publicly insulting the dignity of a holy God? The news editor gave his answer. God gave a different one. If the Old Testament laws were in effect today, every television network executive would have long ago been executed.

We cannot deny that the New Testament seems to reduce the number of capital offenses. By comparison the Old Testament seems radically severe. What we fail to remember, however, is that the Old Testament list represents a massive reduction in capital crimes from the original list. The Old Testament code represents a bending over backward of divine patience and forbearance. The Old Testament Law is one of astonishing grace.

Astonishing grace? I will say it again. The Old Testament list of capital crimes represents a massive reduction of the original list. It is an astonishing measure of grace. The Old Testament record is chiefly a record of the grace of God.

How so? To make sense out of my strange words, we must go back to the beginning, to the original rules of the universe. What was the penalty for sin in the original created order? "The soul who sins is the one who will die" (Ezek. 18:4). In creation all sin is deemed worthy of death. Every sin is a capital offense.

In creation God is not obliged to give us the gift of life. He is not in debt to us. The gift of life comes by His grace and stands under His divine authority. The task that is given to mankind in creation is to bear witness to the holiness of God, to be His image bearer. We are made to mirror and reflect the holiness of God. We are made to be His ambassadors.

God put Adam and Eve on probation and said, "If you sin, you will die." Sin brings the loss of the gift of life. The right to life is forfeited by sin. Once people sin, they forfeit any claim on God to human existence. Now the big question: When was the penalty for sin to be meted out in creation? Was the penalty stated like this: "If you sin, then someday you will die"? No! The penalty for sin was clearly stated by God: "When you eat of it you will surely die" (Gen. 2:17).

In creation the penalty for sin was not only death, but instant death. Death that very day: death as swiftly as it fell on Nadab and Abihu; death as sudden as it wiped out Uzzah; death as quick as it befell Ananias and Sapphira. "The day that you sin you will surely die."

Numerous commentators have tried to soften the divine warning by interpreting the "death" of Genesis 2 as a kind of spiritual death. That is not what the text says. The death penalty of which God warned was real death, death in the full sense of the word. To be sure, Adam and Eve did suffer spiritual death that very day, but God granted mercy in terms of the full measure of the penalty. We have a saying that "justice delayed is justice denied." Not always. In the case of creation and mankind's fall, the full measure of justice was delayed so grace would have time to work. Here the delay of justice was not the denial of justice but the establishing of mercy and grace.

Yet the death penalty was imposed and is still imposed. All people die. We may live out our three score and ten and then die. But die we shall, because we are all under the death penalty for sin. We are all sitting on death row awaiting execution. The greatest mass killer of all time was not Adolf Hitler or Joseph Stalin. The greatest mass killer of all is nature. Everyone falls victim to nature, which does not operate independently from God. Nature is merely the avenger of a holy God.

Was it unjust for God to say to Adam and Eve that they would die when they sinned? Think about it. Was it evil for God to impose the death penalty for all sin? If you say yes, be careful. If you say yes, you are saying it as an expression of the very fallen, sinful nature that exposes you to the death penalty in the first place. If you say yes, you slander the character of God. If you say yes, you do violence to His holiness. If you say yes, you assail the righteous Judge of all the earth. If you say yes, you have never come to grips with what sin is. We must not say yes. We must say no and say it with conviction.

Is the death penalty for sin unjust? By no means. Remember that God voluntarily created us. He gave us the highest privilege of being His image bearers.

He made us but a little lower than the angels. He freely gave us dominion over all the earth. We are not turtles. We are not fireflies. We are not caterpillars or coyotes. We are people. We are the image bearers of the holy and majestic King of the cosmos.

We have not used the gift of life for the purpose God intended. Life on this planet has become the arena in which we daily carry out the work of cosmic treason. Our crime is far more serious, far more destructive than that of Benedict Arnold. No traitor to any king or nation has even approached the wickedness of our treason before God.

Sin is cosmic treason. Sin is treason against a perfectly pure Sovereign. It is an act of supreme ingratitude toward the One to whom we owe everything, to the One who has given us life itself. Have you ever considered the deeper implications of the slightest sin, of the most minute peccadillo? What are we saying to our Creator when we disobey Him at the slightest point? We are saying no to the righteousness of God. We are saying, "God, Your law is not good. My judgment is better than Yours. Your authority does not apply to me. I am above and beyond Your jurisdiction. I have the right to do what I want to do, not what You command me to do."

The slightest sin is an act of defiance against cosmic authority. It is a revolutionary act, a rebellious act in which we are setting ourselves in opposition to the One to whom we owe everything. It is an insult to His holiness. We become false witnesses to God. When we sin as the image bearers of God, we are saying to the whole creation, to all of nature under our dominion, to the birds of the air and the beasts of the field: "This is how God is. This is how your Creator behaves. Look in this mirror; look at us, and you will see the character of the Almighty." We say to the world, "God is covetous; God is ruthless; God is bitter; God is a murderer, a thief, a slanderer, an adulterer. God is all of these things that we are doing."

When people join together in sin, they "speak of kings and things." It is the ultimate conspiracy. We reach for the crown and plot for the throne, saying in effect to God, "We will not have You rule over us." The psalmist put it this way: "Why do the nations conspire and the peoples plot in vain? The kings of the earth take their stand and the rulers gather together against the LORD and against his Anointed One. 'Let us break their chains,' they say, 'and throw off their fetters'" (Ps. 2:1-3).

When we sin, we not only commit treason against God, but we also do violence to each other. Sin violates people. There is nothing abstract about it. By my sin I hurt human beings. I injure their person; I despoil their goods; I impair their reputation; I rob from them a precious quality of life; I crush their dreams and aspirations for happiness. When I dishonor God, I dishonor all people who bear His image. Is it any wonder, then, that God takes sin so seriously?

Hans Küng, the controversial Roman Catholic theologian, writing about the seemingly harsh judgments of sin God makes in the Old Testament, says that the most mysterious aspect of the mystery of sin is not that the sinner deserves to die, but rather that the sinner in the average situation continues to exist.

Küng asks the right question. The issue is not why does God punish sin but why does He permit the on-going human rebellion? What prince, what king, what ruler would display so much patience with a continually rebellious populace?

The key to Küng's observation is that he speaks of sinners' continuing to live in the average situation. That is, it is customary or usual for God to be forbearing. He is indeed long-suffering, patient, and slow to anger. In fact He is so slow to anger that when His anger does erupt, we are shocked and offended by it. We forget rather quickly that God's patience is designed to lead us to repentance, to give us time to be redeemed. Instead of taking advantage of this patience by coming humbly to Him for forgiveness, we use this grace as an opportunity to become more bold in our sin. We delude ourselves into thinking that either God doesn't care about it, or that He is powerless to punish us.

The supreme folly is that we think we will get away with our revolt.

Far from being a history of a harsh God, the Old Testament is the record of a God who is patient in the extreme. The Old Testament is the history of a persistently stiff-necked people who rebel time after time against God. The people became slaves in a foreign land. They cried out to God. God heard their groans and moved to redeem them. He parted the Red Sea to let them out of bondage. They responded by worshiping a golden calf.

We must still face the difficult question of the

conquest of Canaan. There God explicitly commanded the slaughter of men, women, and children. The Promised Land was given to Israel by a bloody sword, a sword dripping with the blood of infants and women. God directly issued the order for the bloodbath:

> When the LORD your God brings you into the land you are entering to possess and drives out before you many nations—the Hittites, Girgashites, Amorites, Canaanites, Perizzites, Hivites and Jebusites, seven nations larger and stronger than you—and when the LORD your God has delivered them over to you and you have defeated them, then you must destroy them totally. Make no treaty with them, and show them no mercy. (Deut. 7:1-2)

Why did God issue such a command? How could He have ordered the slaughter of women and children? Again we find modern attempts to soften the event. A curriculum for high school students prepared by a major church denomination in the United States explained that in light of the New Testament revelation of God's love, we know that God did not ever issue such a belligerent command. The Old Testament is merely the record of a primitive warlike group of Hebrews who tried to justify ruthless policies by attributing them to a divine sanction.

The writers of the curriculum did not believe that God ever issued such a command. It was to be a case of intrusion of mythology into the biblical record.

Such interpretations overlook some vital aspects of the matter. First, there is a historical precedent that is far more severe than the conquest of Canaan—the Flood. In the Flood God destroyed the entire population of the world except for Noah and his family. The Flood was a "conquest of Canaan" on a grand scale. More important is the failure to understand the nature of sin. The assumption of the commentators is that God wiped out innocent people in Canaan. Of the multitudes of women and children living in Canaan, none was innocent. The conquest of Canaan was an explicit expression of God's righteous judgment on a wicked nation. He made that point clear to Israel. He also made it clear to the people of Israel that they also were not innocent. It was not as if God destroyed a wicked people for the sake of a righteous people. To the Canaanites God poured out justice. To the Jews God poured out mercy. He was quick to remind the Jews of that:

> After the LORD your God has driven them out before you, do not say to yourself, "The LORD has brought me here to take possession of this land because of my righteousness." No, it is on account of the wickedness of these nations that the LORD is going to drive them out before you. It is not because of your righteousness or your integrity that you are going in to take possession of their land; but on account of the wickedness of these nations, the LORD your God will drive them out before you, to accomplish what he swore

to your fathers, to Abraham, Isaac and Jacob.
Understand, then, that it is not because of
your righteousness that the LORD your God is
giving you this good land to possess, for you
are a stiff-necked people. (Deut. 9:4-6)

Three times in this passage God reminded the people of Israel that it was not because of their righteousness that He would defeat the Canaanites. He wanted to
make that point clear. Israel might have been tempted
to jump to the conclusion that God was "on their side"
because they were better than pagan nations. God's announcement made that inference impossible.

The holiness of God is at the heart of the issue of
the conquest of Canaan. It was because of His holiness
that the act was ordained. On the one hand He moved
to punish the insult to His holiness that was daily per-
petrated by the Canaanites. On the other hand He
was preparing a land and a nation for a holy purpose.
God commanded that no mercy be shown toward the
inhabitants of the land. He explained why:

Do not intermarry with them. Do not give
your daughters to their sons or take their
daughters for your sons, for they will turn your
sons away from following me to serve other
gods, and the LORD's anger will burn against
you and will quickly destroy you. This is what
you are to do to them: Break down their altars,
smash their sacred stones, cut down their
Asherah poles and burn their idols in the fire.
For you are a people holy to the LORD your

God. The LORD your God has chosen you
out of all the peoples on the face of the earth
to be his people, his treasured possession.
(Deut. 7:3-6)

God did not choose Israel because Israel was already holy. He chose them to *make* them holy. Israel
was called to be holy in two senses of the word. They
were called to be different, to be set apart as a vehicle
of God's plan of redemption. They were also called to
be holy in the sense of being purified. Pagan practices
were to be absent from Israel's midst. They were to
be sanctified by drawing near to God. Salvation for
the nations was to come out of Israel. The Promised
Land was to be the breeding ground for the coming
Messiah. There was no room for pagan shrines and
pagan rites. God ordained a scorched-earth policy to
purge the land for future salvation.

We have labored the problems of the acts of divine
justice found in the Old Testament. We have tried to
show that God's justice was neither whimsical nor
unwarranted. We must add that there is no real conflict between the God of the Old Testament and the
God of the New Testament. It was the Old Testament
God whom Christ called "Father." It was the God of
Abraham, Isaac, and Jacob who so loved the world
that He sent His one and only Son to redeem it. It
was Jesus' meat and drink to do the will of this God.
It was zeal for the God who slew Nadab, Abihu, and
Uzzah that consumed Christ. It was the God who de-
stroyed the world by a flood who pours the waters of
His grace out to us.

The false conflict between the two testaments may be seen in the most brutal act of divine vengeance ever recorded in Scripture. It is not found in the Old Testament but in the New Testament. The most violent expression of God's wrath and justice is seen in the Cross. If ever a person had room to complain of injustice, it was Jesus. He was the only innocent man ever to be punished by God. If we stagger at the wrath of God, let us stagger at the Cross. Here is where our astonishment should be focused. If we have cause for moral outrage, let it be directed at Golgotha.

The Cross was at once the most horrible and the most beautiful example of God's wrath. It was the most just and the most gracious act in history. God would have been more than unjust, He would have been diabolical to punish Jesus if Jesus had not first willingly taken on Himself the sins of the world. Once Christ had done that, once He volunteered to be the Lamb of God, laden with our sin, then He became the most grotesque and vile thing on this planet. With the concentrated load of sin He carried, He became utterly repugnant to the Father. God poured out His wrath on this obscene thing. God made Christ accursed for the sin He bore. Herein was God's holy justice perfectly manifest. Yet it was done for us. He took what justice demanded from us. This "for us" aspect of the Cross is what displays the majesty of its grace. At the same time justice and grace, wrath and mercy. It is too astonishing to fathom.

We cringe at God's justice because its expression is so unusual. As Küng observed, God's usual course of action is one of grace. Grace no longer amazes us. We have grown used to it; we take it for granted.

Perhaps the best illustration of this may be found in the teaching of Jesus:

> Now there were some present at that time who told Jesus about the Galileans whose blood Pilate had mixed with their sacrifices. Jesus answered, "Do you think that these Galileans were worse sinners than all the other Galileans because they suffered this way? I tell you, no! But unless you repent, you too will all perish. Or those eighteen who died when the tower in Siloam fell on them—do you think they were more guilty than all the others living in Jerusalem? I tell you, no! But unless you repent, you too will all perish." (Luke 13:1-5)

This is one of the most difficult of the "hard sayings" of Jesus. The question is raised, What about the people Pilate slaughtered, or the innocent people killed by the falling of the tower? Where was God in these events? The question under discussion was, How could God allow these things to happen? The question is actually a thinly veiled accusation. The issue was, as always, How can God allow innocent people to suffer?

We can hear the implied protest in the question. The eighteen innocent people were walking down the street minding their own business. They were not engaged in playing "sidewalk superintendent." They were not heckling the construction workers.

They were not running away after robbing a bank. They just were "there," at the wrong time and in the wrong place. They suffered the consequences of a fatal accident.

Note Jesus' response. He did not say, "I am very sorry to hear about this tragedy. These things happen, and there is not much we can do about it. It was fate. An accident. As good Christians you have to learn to accept the bad with the good. Keep a stiff upper lip. Be good Stoics! I know I taught you that the One who keeps Israel neither slumbers nor sleeps. But that was a poetic statement, a bit of hyperbole. Do you realize what a difficult task it is for My Father to run the universe? It gets tiring. Every now and then He must take a nap. On the afternoon in question He was very weary and grabbed forty winks. While He was nodding, the tower fell. I am sorry about that, and I will report your grievance to Him. I will ask Him to be a bit more careful in the future."

Jesus did not say, "I know I told you that My Father notices the landing of every sparrow and that He numbers the hairs on your head. Do you realize how many sparrows there are flying around? And the hairs on your head! The afternoon the tower fell, my Father was busy counting the hairs on the head of a particularly bushy-haired fellow. He was concentrating so hard on the fellow's head that He overlooked the falling tower. I will suggest that He get His priorities in order and not spend so much time with sparrows and hair."

No. Instead, Jesus rebuked the people for putting their amazement in the wrong place. He said, "Unless you repent, you too will all perish." In effect what Jesus was saying was this: "You people are asking the wrong question. You should be asking me, 'Why didn't that tower fall on my head?'"

In two decades of teaching theology, I have had countless students ask me why God doesn't save everybody. Only once did a student come to me and say, "There is something I just can't figure out. Why did God redeem *me*?"

We are not really surprised that God has redeemed us. Somewhere deep inside, in the secret chambers of our hearts, we harbor the notion that God owes us His mercy. Heaven would not be quite the same if we were excluded from it. We know that we are sinners, but we are surely not as bad as we could be. There are enough redeeming features to our personalities that if God is really just, He will include us in salvation. What amazes us is justice, not grace.

Our tendency to take grace for granted was powerfully demonstrated while I was teaching college students. I had the assignment of teaching a freshman Old Testament course to 250 students at a Christian college. On the first day of class I went over the course assignments carefully. My experience taught me that the assignment of term papers required a special degree of explanation. This course required three short papers. I explained to the students that the first paper was due on my desk by noon the last day of September. No extensions were to be given except for students who were physically confined to the infirmary or who had deaths in the immediate family. If the paper was not turned in on time, the student would receive an F for the assignment. The students acknowledged that they understood the requirements.

On the last day of September, 225 students dutifully handed in their term papers. Twenty-five students stood, quaking in terror, full of remorse. They cried out, "Oh, Professor Sproul. We are so sorry. We didn't budget our time properly. We didn't make the proper adjustment from high school to college. Please don't give us an F. Please, oh, please give us an extension."

I bowed to their pleas for mercy. "All right," I said. "I'll give you a break this time. But, remember, the next assignment is due the last day of October."

The students were profuse in their gratitude and filled the air with solemn promises of being on time for the next assignment. Then came the last day of October. Two hundred students came with their papers. Fifty students came empty-handed. They were nervous but not in panic. When I asked for their papers, again they were contrite. "Oh, Professor. It was Homecoming Week. Besides it is midterm, and all of our assignments are due in other classes. Please give us one more chance. We promise it will never happen again."

Once more I relented. I said, "Okay, but this is the last time. If you are late for the next paper, it will be an F. No excuses, no whining. F. Is that clear?"

"Oh, yes, Professor. You are terrific." Spontaneously the class began to sing, "We love you, Prof Sproul. Oh, yes we do." I was Mr. Popularity.

Can you guess what happened on the last day of November? Right. One hundred and fifty students came with their term papers. The other hundred strolled into the lecture hall utterly unconcerned. "Where are your term papers?" I asked.

One student replied, "Oh, don't worry, Prof, we're working on them. We'll have them for you in a couple of days, no sweat."

I picked up my lethal black grade book and began taking down names. "Johnson! Do you have your paper?"

"No sir" came the reply.

"F," I said as I wrote the grade in the book. "Muldaney! Do you have your paper?"

Again, "No sir" was the reply. I marked another F in the book.

The students reacted with unmitigated fury. They howled in protest, screaming, "That's not fair!"

I looked at one of the howling students. "Lavery! You think it's not fair?"

"Yes," he growled in response.

"I see. It's justice you want? I seem to recall that you were late with your paper the last time. If you insist on justice, you will certainly get it. I'll not only give you an F for this assignment, but I'll change your last grade to the F you so richly deserved."

The student was stunned. He had no more arguments to make. He apologized for being so hasty and was suddenly happy to settle for one F instead of two.

The students had quickly taken my mercy for granted. They assumed it. When justice suddenly fell, they were unprepared for it. It came as a shock, and they were outraged. This, after only two doses of mercy in the space of two months.

The normal activity of God involves far more mercy than I showed those students with their term papers. Old Testament history covers hundreds of years. In that time God was repeatedly merciful. When His divine judgment fell on Nadab or Uzzah, the response was shock and outrage. We have come to expect God to be merciful. From there the next step is easy: We demand it. When it is not forthcoming, our first response is anger against God, coupled with the protest: "It isn't fair." We soon forget that with our first sin we have forfeited all rights to the gift of life. That I am drawing breath this morning is an act of divine mercy. God owes me nothing. I owe Him everything. If He allows a tower to fall on my head this afternoon, I cannot claim injustice.

One of our basic problems is the confusion of justice and mercy. We live in a world where injustices happen. They happen among people. Every one of us at some time has been a victim of injustice at the hands of another person. Every one of us at some time has committed an injustice against another person. People treat each other unfairly. One thing is certain: No matter how much injustice I have suffered from the hands of other people, I have never suffered the slightest injustice from the hand of God.

Suppose a person falsely accuses me of stealing money. Charges are brought against me, and I am arrested and sent to prison. On the human level, I have been a victim of gross injustice. I have every right to cry out to God and plead for vindication in this world. I can complain about being falsely persecuted. God is angry with people for unjustly putting me in prison. God promises to vindicate me from this injustice someday. Injustice is real, and it happens every day in this world.

The injustices we suffer are all of a *horizontal* sort. They happen between actors in this world. Yet standing over and above this world is the Great Judge of all. My relationship to Him is vertical. In terms of that vertical relationship I never suffer an injustice. Though people may mistreat me, God never does. That God allows a human being to treat me unjustly is just of God. While I may complain to God about the human, horizontal injustice I have suffered, I cannot rise up and accuse God of committing a vertical injustice by allowing the human injustice to befall me. God would be perfectly just to allow me to be thrown in prison for life for a crime I didn't commit. I may be innocent before other people, but I am guilty before God.

We often blame God for the injustices done to us and harbor in our souls the bitter feeling that God has not been fair toward us. Even if we recognize that He is gracious, we think that He has not been gracious enough. We think we deserve more grace.

Please read that last sentence again: *We think we deserve more grace.* What is wrong with that sentence? Grammatically it is fine. But there is something seriously wrong with the content, with the meaning of the sentence.

It is impossible for anyone, anywhere, anytime to *deserve* grace. Grace by definition is undeserved. As soon as we talk about deserving something, we are no longer talking about grace; we are talking about justice. Only justice can be deserved. God is never obligated to be merciful. Mercy and grace must be voluntary or they are no longer mercy and grace. God never "owes" grace. He reminds us more than once: "I will have mercy on whom I will have mercy" (Exod. 33:19). This is the divine prerogative. God reserves for Himself the supreme right of executive clemency.

Suppose ten people sin and sin equally. Suppose God punishes five of them and is merciful to the other five. Is this injustice? No! In this situation five people get justice and five get mercy. No one gets injustice. What we tend to assume is this: If God is merciful to five, He must be equally merciful to the other five. Why? He is never obligated to be merciful. If He is merciful to nine of the ten, the tenth cannot claim to be a victim of injustice. God never owes mercy. God is not obliged to treat all people equally. Maybe I'd better say that again. *God is never obliged to treat all people equally.* If He were ever unjust to us, we would have reason to complain. But simply because He grants mercy to my neighbor, it gives me no claim on His mercy. Again we must remember that mercy is always voluntary. "I will have mercy on whom I will have mercy."

I will receive only justice or mercy from God. I never receive injustice from His hand. We may request that God help us get justice at the hands of other people, but we would be utterly foolish ever to ask Him for justice from Himself. I warn my students: "Don't ever ask God for justice—you might get it."

It is the confusion between justice and mercy that

makes us shrink in horror when we read the stories of Nadab, Abihu, and Uzzah. When God's justice falls, we are offended because we think God owes perpetual mercy. We must not take His grace for granted. We must never lose our capacity to be amazed by grace. We sing the song, "Amazing Justice." Our lyrics tend to go like this:

Amazing Justice, cruel and sharp
That wounds a saint like me:
I'm so darn good it makes no sense—
The tower fell on me!

I remember preaching a "practice sermon" in preaching class in seminary. In my sermon I was extolling the marvels of God's grace. As the hymn says, I spoke of "God's grace, infinite grace."

At the end of my sermon the professor had a question for me. "Mr. Sproul," he said, "where did you ever get the idea that God's grace is infinite? Is there absolutely no limit to His grace?" As soon as he asked that question, I knew I was in trouble. I could quote him chapter and verse of the hymn that taught me that, but somehow I couldn't come up with a single Scripture verse that taught God's grace is infinite.

The reason I couldn't find any Scripture passage to support my statement is because there is none. God's grace is not infinite. God is infinite, and God is gracious. We experience the grace of an infinite God, but grace is not infinite. God sets limits to His patience and forbearance. He warns us over and over again that someday the ax will fall and His judgment will be poured out.

Since it is our tendency to take grace for granted, my guess is that God found it necessary from time to time to remind Israel that grace must never be assumed. On rare but dramatic occasions He showed the dreadful power of His justice. He killed Nadab and Abihu. He killed Uzzah. He commanded the slaughter of the Canaanites. It is as if He were saying, "Be careful. While you enjoy the benefits of My grace, don't forget My justice. Don't forget the gravity of sin. Remember that I am holy."

Allowing God's Holiness to Touch Our Lives

As you reflect about what you have learned and rediscovered about God's holiness, answer these questions. Use a journal to record your responses to God's holiness, or discuss your responses with a friend.

1. In what ways does God's justice frighten you? In what ways does it comfort you?
2. What is your response when you realize that you deserve to die because of your sin?
3. What is your response when you realize that God's justice demanded Christ's death for you?
4. In what ways has God demonstrated His mercy to you?

SEVEN

War and Peace with a Holy God

If man is not made for God,

why is he only happy in God?

If man is made for God,

why is he so opposed to God?

BLAISE PASCAL

The biblical record contains the stories of men and women who have wrestled with God. The very name *Israel* means "one who struggles with God." God is holy. He is high above us, transcendent. Yet He is a God with whom we can wrestle. In our wrestling match the goal is not final war but final peace. Some have found it. In this chapter we will look at examples of people who have gone to the mat with God and come away at peace. We will look at Jacob, Job, Habakkuk, and Saul of Tarsus. Then we will examine what it means to make peace with God.

Jacob was a rascal. His name means "supplanter." He was the fellow who deceived his father, conned his brother, and entered into an ungodly conspiracy with his mother. It is hard to imagine that the son of Isaac and the grandson of Abraham could be so corrupt. But in the course of Jacob's life, he underwent a radical transformation. It started at Bethel: "Jacob left Beersheba and set out for Haran. When he reached a certain place, he stopped for the night because the sun had set. Taking one of the stones there, he put it under his head and lay down to sleep" (Gen. 28:10-11).

Travel in ancient Palestine was often an ordeal. Night brought danger from marauding thieves and wild beasts. On Jacob's journey there was no way station for him to seek lodging. He traveled as far as he could until the sun went down. At that point he made camp under the stars. His pillow for the night was a stone. When he settled into sleep, he had a dream that was destined to change his life:

> He had a dream in which he saw a stairway resting on the earth, with its top reaching to heaven, and the angels of God were ascending and descending on it. There above it stood the LORD, and he said: "I am the LORD, the God of your father Abraham and the God of Isaac. I will give you and your descendants the land on which you are lying. Your descendants will be like the dust of the earth, and you will spread out to the west and to the east, to the north and to the south. All peoples on earth will be blessed through you and your offspring. I am with you and will watch over you wherever you go, and I will bring you back to this land. I will not leave you until I have done what I have promised you." (Gen. 28:12-15)

The stairway Jacob saw in his dream is commonly referred to as "Jacob's ladder." It served as a bridge between heaven and earth. Up to this point in his life Jacob was not in touch with heavenly things. He had a profound sense of the *absence of God*. It seems strange that a son of Isaac and grandson of Abraham would be so "secular." Abraham had spoken with God. Surely young Jacob had sat around campfires and heard stories from his father and grandfather. He must have known about God's order to Abraham to sacrifice Isaac on an altar at Mount Moriah.

Jacob's life had been lived out on the plane of this world. Talk about heavenly matters had made little impression on him. His mind was fixed on the earth. As far as he was concerned, there was an unbridgeable chasm between heaven and earth. If there was a God, He was so remote, so utterly transcendent that He had no relevance to Jacob's life. This God of whom his parents spoke was too high for Jacob to reach— until he had a dream.

The dream featured a stairway. The stairway was a contact point, a connection between the realm of the holy and the realm of the profane. On the stairway Jacob saw angels ascending and descending. They were moving in both directions, from earth to heaven and from heaven to earth. The traffic was continuous. They moved from his presence to God's presence. At the top of the staircase Jacob saw the figure of God. God spoke to him, confirming the promise that He had made earlier to Abraham and Isaac. The promise of God would continue to future generations. It was going to pass through Jacob. He would be the carrier of the covenant oath that God had sworn. God promised to be with Jacob wherever he went and to stay with him until all the promises had been accomplished.

Whatever happened to Jacob's ladder? The image virtually disappears in Old Testament history. Centuries pass with no mention of it. Then suddenly, it appears again in the New Testament:

> Philip found Nathanael and told him, "We have found the one Moses wrote about in the Law, and about whom the prophets also wrote—Jesus of Nazareth, the son of Joseph."
>
> "Nazareth! Can anything good come from there?" Nathanael asked.
>
> "Come and see," said Philip.
>
> When Jesus saw Nathanael approaching, he said of him, "Here is a true Israelite, in whom there is nothing false."
>
> "How do you know me?" Nathanael asked.
>
> Jesus answered, "I saw you while you were still under the fig tree before Philip called you."
>
> Then Nathanael declared, "Rabbi, you are the Son of God; you are the King of Israel."
>
> Jesus said, "You believe because I told you I saw you under the fig tree. You shall see greater things than that." He then added, "I tell you the truth, you shall see heaven open, and the angels of God ascending and descending on the Son of Man." (John 1:45-51)

Jesus' words to Nathanael were radical. In this conversation He declared that He is the ladder of Jacob; He is the bridge between heaven and earth; He is the one who spans the chasm between the Transcendent

One and mere humans. The angels of God ascend and descend on Him. He makes the absent God present among us. Was this what Jacob saw in a dim, shadowy way?

When Jacob awoke from his dream, he was stunned. He was overcome by the power of his nighttime vision. "When Jacob awoke from his sleep, he thought, 'Surely the LORD is in this place, and I was not aware of it.' He was afraid and said, 'How awesome is this place! This is none other than the house of God; this is the gate of heaven'" (Gen. 28:16-17).

The name of the place where Jacob had his dream became known as Bethel. In Hebrew, the word *Bethel* means "house of God." There was no tabernacle there, no temple, no church. Jacob called it the house of God because there the Holy One made Himself known. Jacob's words are typical of the plight contemporary culture feels. Ours is a day when people feel a sense of the absence of God. We see no burning bushes, no pillars of fire, no incarnate Christ walking in our midst. We feel abandoned, thrown to the waters of a hostile or, even worse, indifferent universe. We seem locked into a world from which there is no exit, no stairway to the stars.

Jacob felt the same way until he had his dream. His words are relevant to our modern situation. "Surely the LORD is in this place, and I was not aware of it." God was there all the time. He was not remote from Jacob, but Jacob had missed Him all of his life. Jacob was unaware of the presence of God. This tragic ignorance of God's presence is played out in our culture every day in the lives of millions of people. God is here, but we are unaware. The moment awareness of His divine presence begins, the deepest personal struggle a person can experience begins as well. The dream did not end Jacob's struggle. It was the beginning of a struggle that was for keeps. From that moment on, he was fighting for his own soul.

"How awesome is this place!" This was Jacob's response to being in the house of God. People do not normally feel that way in church. There is no sense of awe, no sense of being in the presence of One who makes us tremble. People in awe never complain that church is boring.

Scholars do not agree on the precise time of Jacob's conversion. Some locate it here at Bethel, when he had the overwhelming sense of God's presence. Others pinpoint it years later in Jacob's life when he had his fateful wrestling match with God:

> That night Jacob got up and took his two wives, his two maidservants and his eleven sons and crossed the ford of the Jabbok. After he had sent them across the stream, he sent over all his possessions. So Jacob was left alone, and a man wrestled with him till daybreak. When the man saw that he could not overpower him, he touched the socket of Jacob's hip so that his hip was wrenched as he wrestled with the man. Then the man said, "Let me go, for it is daybreak."

> But Jacob replied, "I will not let you go unless you bless me."

The man asked him, "What is your name?"

"Jacob," he answered.

Then the man said, "Your name will no longer be Jacob, but Israel, because you have struggled with God and with men and have overcome."

Jacob said, "Please tell me your name."

But he replied, "Why do you ask my name?" Then he blessed him there.

So Jacob called the place Peniel, saying, "It is because I saw God face to face, and yet my life was spared." (Gen. 32:22-30)

Obviously the "man" Jacob wrestled was more than a man—he was the angel of God. The battle was fierce, raging through the night with neither combatant gaining the upper hand. Finally the angel used the overpowering might of God to touch the socket of Jacob's hip. Jacob's "victory" was not one of conquest but of survival. He walked away from the duel, but he walked with a limp for the rest of his life.

The discussion with the angel about names is significant. The angel demanded the name of Jacob. The demand for the name was similar to the custom we have today of indicating surrender by saying "uncle." For the combatant to yield his name meant that he was acknowledging the superiority of the other party. The yielding of the name was an act of submission. When Jacob surrendered his name, he surrendered his soul. He relinquished authority over his own life. With the surrender came a new name, a new identity. *Israel.*

In defeat Jacob was still hoping for a draw, a tie that would leave his pride intact. Even a split decision would help. He said to the angel, "Please tell me your name." Note the difference in the name-exchange issue. The angel demanded Jacob's name, and Jacob surrendered it. Jacob politely requested the angel's name and did not get it. This was the final act of divine conquest. There are no draws with God, no split decisions. When we wrestle with the Almighty, we lose. He is the undefeated champion of the universe.

The Holy One cannot be defeated in personal combat. But there is some consolation here. Jacob wrestled with God and lived. He was beaten. He was left crippled, but he survived that battle. At least we can learn from this that God will engage us in our honest struggles. We may wrestle with the Holy One. Indeed, for the transforming power of God to change our lives, we must wrestle with Him. We must know what it means to fight with God all night if we are also to know what it means to experience the sweetness of the soul's surrender.

No one ever carried on a livelier, more strident debate with God than did Job. If ever a man seemed to have a right to challenge God, it was Job. Job had been declared righteous by God Himself, and still he was afflicted with immeasurable misery. The drama of Job makes it seem as if the poor man was nothing more than a pawn in a cosmic struggle between

God and Satan. God allowed Job to be put to a test. His possessions were stolen; his family was destroyed; and finally he was afflicted with a tormenting scourge of boils. He found no relief from his pain. His bodily anguish soon affected his soul.

I once talked to an elderly woman who was battling cancer with chemotherapy. She suffered the side effects of nausea from the treatments. I asked her how her spirits were holding up, and she offered a most candid reply: "It is hard to be a Christian when your head is in the toilet." The woman understood the close connection between body and soul. It is extremely difficult to be spiritual when the body is afflicted with unremitting pain.

Yet Job did not blaspheme. He cried out, "Though he slay me, yet will I hope in him" (Job 13:15). Even his wife tried to get him to find ultimate relief. Her advice was simple and to the point: "Curse God and die!" (Job 2:9).

Job refused to take the easy way out. He suffered the counsel of fools by listening to the advice of his friends. Finally he rose up to challenge God on the matter. He faced God alone, wrestling and struggling for answers to his misery. God's reply was hardly comforting:

> Then the LORD answered Job out of the storm. He said: "Who is this that darkens my counsel with words without knowledge? Brace yourself like a man; I will question you, and you shall answer me. Where were you when I laid the earth's foundation? Tell me, if you understand.

Who marked off its dimensions? Surely you know! Who stretched a measuring line across it? On what were its footings set, or who laid its cornerstone—while the morning stars sang together and all the angels shouted for joy? Who shut up the sea behind doors when it burst forth from the womb, when I made the clouds its garment and wrapped it in thick darkness, when I fixed limits for it and set its doors and bars in place, when I said, 'This far you may come and no farther; here is where your proud waves halt'?" (Job 38:1-11)

This was a very difficult oral examination. Job demanded answers from God. Instead of answers he received a bundle of questions in return. God rebuked Job for casting a dark shadow over divine wisdom by his own ignorance. It was as if God said, "Okay, Job, you want to interrogate me? Fine, I'll answer your questions, but first I have a few for you." Like bullets from a rapid-fire machine gun, God shot out questions, each one more intimidating than the last. Finally Job spoke: "Then Job answered the LORD: 'I am unworthy—how can I reply to you? I put my hand over my mouth. I spoke once, but I have no answer—twice, but I will say no more'" (Job 40:3-5).

Consider the image Job used. He said that he would place his hand over his mouth. He gagged himself. He covered his lips with his hand lest any more foolish words escape his mouth. He was sorry that he ever challenged God. He recognized that his words had been presumptuous. He had said all he wanted to say.

But the interrogation continued. God was not yet finished with the examination. He asked a series of questions that overwhelmed Job: "Would you discredit my justice? Would you condemn me to justify yourself?" (Job 40:8).

Here the issue is plain. Job's challenge flies into the teeth of divine justice. His charges are an insult to a holy God. God's question rings in Job's ears: "Will you condemn me to justify yourself?" There is no doubt that Job longed to be justified. He was sick of the accusations of his friends. He did not understand why he was so miserable. He prayed for vindication. But his desire had gone out of control. He was on the verge of trading God's justification for his own. He had crossed a line in the debate, suggesting that perhaps God had done evil. God asked him straight out, "Do you want to condemn me so that you can be exonerated?"

The full weight of God's questions fell hard on Job. He was almost crushed by them. Finally he took his hand away from his mouth and spoke again. This time there were no accusations in his words. He broke his vow of silence only to voice his contrition:

> I know that you can do all things; no plan of yours can be thwarted. You asked, "Who is this that obscures my counsel without knowledge?" Surely I spoke of things I did not understand, things too wonderful for me to know. You said, "Listen now, and I will speak; I will question you, and you shall answer me." My ears had heard of you but now my eyes have seen you.

Therefore I despise myself and repent in dust and ashes. (Job 42:2-6)

When we read this section of the book of Job, we may get the idea that God was bullying Job. He cried out for answers, and God said that He would answer Job's questions. But the answers never came forth. To be sure, there was a condition attached to the promise of answers: Job was required to answer first. But Job flunked his exam. God then gave no answers.

Yet Job was satisfied. Even though God gave no answers, Job's questions were put to rest. He received a higher answer than any direct reply could have provided. God answered Job's questions not with words but with Himself. As soon as Job saw who God is, Job was satisfied. Seeing the manifestation of God was all that he needed. He was able to leave the details in God's hands. Once God Himself was no longer shrouded in mystery, Job was able to live comfortably with a few unanswered questions. When God appeared, Job was so busy repenting that he did not have time for further challenges. His rage was redirected to himself: "I despise myself and repent in dust and ashes."

We point now to one more Old Testament man who challenged God. The prophet Habakkuk took God to task for doing things that offended his sense of justice. The prophet was appalled that God's people should suffer at the hands of a nation that was more wicked than they were themselves. On the surface it looked as if God had abandoned His promises to the Jews and had become a turncoat, giving His divine allegiance to the wicked Babylonians. For Habakkuk this was comparable to a modern-day Jew wondering if God was on Hitler's side during the Holocaust. Habakkuk's complaint was registered with a loud protest:

> How long, O LORD, must I call for help,
> but you do not listen? Or cry out to you,
> "Violence!" but you do not save? Why do
> you make me look at injustice? Why do you
> tolerate wrong? Destruction and violence
> are before me; there is strife, and conflict
> abounds. Therefore the law is paralyzed, and
> justice never prevails. The wicked hem in
> the righteous, so that justice is perverted.
> (Hab. 1:2-4)

Habakkuk was flaming angry. His complaint was so heated that he overdid it a bit. He said, "Justice never prevails." Surely in this world there is injustice that awaits final rectification, but to say that justice *never* prevails is going overboard. Like Job, Habakkuk demanded some answers. He went to the mat with God and was prepared to wrestle it out. He stood in his watchtower, waiting for a reply from the Almighty. When God finally spoke, Habakkuk's reaction was like Job's: "I heard and my heart pounded, my lips quivered at the sound; decay crept into my bones, and my legs trembled" (Hab. 3:16).

The response of the prophet was like that of a small child who is scolded by a parent. His heart palpitated, and his lips began to quiver. We have all seen small children on the verge of tears. They try to hold back the flood, but the tremor in the lower lip gives them away. Here was a grown man whose lips quivered in the presence of God. He felt a kind of internal rottenness, a decay entering his very bones. The skeletal structure of the man felt as if it were collapsing. The trembling of the *mysterium tremendum* attacked his legs; his knees began to knock. He walked away from his wrestling match with God, but he walked on wobbly legs.

With the appearance of God, all of Habakkuk's angry protests ceased. Suddenly the tone of his speech changed from one of bitter despair to one of unwavering confidence and hope: "Though the fig tree does not bud and there are no grapes on the vines, though the olive crop fails and the fields produce no food, though there are no sheep in the pen and no cattle in the stalls, yet I will rejoice in the LORD, I will be joyful in God my Savior" (Hab. 3:17-18).

Habakkuk was now as fierce in his joy as he had been in his despair. He was able to rest absolutely in God's sovereignty. His words, translated into modern jargon, might sound like this: "Even if the budget is never balanced, even if the stock market crashes, even if food prices skyrocket, even if my child never recovers from her illness, even if I lose my job, and even if we lose our home—yet will I rejoice in the God of my salvation."

Jacob, Job, and Habakkuk all declared war on God. They all stormed the battlements of heaven. They were all defeated, yet they all came away from the struggle with uplifted souls. They paid a price in pain. God allowed the debate, but the battle was fierce before peace was established.

Saul of Tarsus felt the same overpowering conquest by God. He was a zealot for the Pharisees, totally repulsed by the advent of a new sect called Christianity. He was determined to wipe Christians from the face of the earth. Commissioned by the authorities, he went from house to house rounding up early Christian believers and casting them into prison. He stood on the sidelines during the stoning of Stephen and applauded the act. He was gleeful when he gained a new assignment to go to Damascus to continue his massacre of Christians. It was on the Damascus Road that he met the Holy One. He recounted the scene during his trial before King Agrippa:

> About noon, O king, as I was on the road,
> I saw a light from heaven, brighter than the
> sun, blazing around me and my companions.
> We all fell to the ground, and I heard a voice
> saying to me in Aramaic, "Saul, Saul, why do
> you persecute me? It is hard for you to kick
> against the goads."

> Then I asked, "Who are you, Lord?"

> "I am Jesus, whom you are persecuting," the
> Lord replied. "Now get up and stand on your
> feet. I have appeared to you to appoint you as a
> servant and as a witness of what you have seen
> of me and what I will show you. I will rescue

you from your own people and from the
Gentiles. I am sending you to them to open
their eyes and turn them from darkness to
light, and from the power of Satan to God, so
that they may receive forgiveness of sins and a
place among those who are sanctified by faith
in me."

So then, King Agrippa, I was not disobedient
to the vision from heaven. (Acts 26:13-19)

Saul was zealous in his pursuit of righteousness.
He was a Pharisee of Pharisees, a man committed to
legal perfection. The irony of his zeal is seen in that
the more zealous he was for his goals, the more opposed he actually became to the work of God. Not
that God is opposed to the pursuit of righteousness.
God is for the pursuit of righteousness, but He stands
against the proud and the arrogant. He stands against
those who are swelled up with self-righteousness.
While Saul was convinced he was fighting for God,
he was actually fighting against God. In this ironic
battle he was doomed to an ultimate confrontation
with the very Christ he opposed.

One of the names by which God is revealed in the
Old Testament is the name *El Shaddai*. The name
means "the thunderer" or "the overpowerer." It was by
the name El Shaddai that God appeared to Job. What
Job experienced was the awesome power of a sovereign God who overpowers all people and is Himself
overpowered by no one. Saul met the Overpowerer
on the road to Damascus.

Saul described his experience on the desert road as starting with the appearance of a dazzling light. The desert road at noonday was a place where the brilliance of the sun was particularly strong, piercing the day through a very thin atmosphere. Under normal conditions the sunshine there is intense. For any other light to be noticed against the backdrop of the desert sun, it must have been extraordinary. Saul spoke of a light more brilliant, more dazzling than the sun. He described it as a "light from heaven."

The expression "light from heaven" does not mean a light from the sky. The sun shines from the sky. Saul was in the presence of the heavenly glory of God. God's glory is the outward manifestation of His holiness. The effulgence of His glory is so scintillating, so brilliant that it eclipses the noonday sun. In the book of Revelation we read of the appearance of the new Jerusalem, the city that comes down from heaven: "I did not see a temple in the city, because the Lord God Almighty and the Lamb are its temple. The city does not need the sun or the moon to shine on it, for the glory of God gives it light, and the Lamb is its lamp" (Rev. 21:22-23).

The new Jerusalem has no sun simply because it has no need for the sun. The glory of God and of His Christ is so bright that the sun itself is overpowered by it. Saul was blinded by its rays. Consider what happens to people if they gaze directly into the sun. In times of solar eclipse people are attracted by the strange sight of a shadow passing over the sun. There is a strong temptation to fix our gaze directly at it. Yet, even in eclipse we find it is painful and dangerous to look directly at the sun. We are warned by the news media at such times not to make attempts to look directly at it, lest we do serious damage to our eyes. If we cannot gaze directly at the sun during an eclipse, how much more severe would be the brilliance that literally outshines the sun? The glory of God reaches a magnitude of brightness far beyond that of the sun shining at full strength.

No angel appeared to wrestle with Saul. Yet some supernatural force threw him to the ground. In an instant Saul was blinded. There was no warning, no whisper of wind to alert him. Sovereignly and powerfully he was knocked flat to the desert floor.

With the light from heaven came also a voice. The voice is elsewhere described as the sound of many waters, a voice that roars like a booming waterfall that is cascading over rocks. Saul identified the voice as speaking in the Aramaic tongue, the native language of Jesus. The voice addressed Saul personally, in the form of the repetition of his name: "Saul, Saul." This double form of address indicated a greeting of personal intimacy. It was the way God addressed Moses at the burning bush and Abraham at his altar on Mount Moriah. It was the form by which Jesus cried over Jerusalem and addressed His Father in His darkest hour on the cross.

"Saul, Saul, why do you persecute me?" Notice that the voice did not inquire why Saul was persecuting Christ's church. It was rather, "Why do you persecute *me*?" To attack the church of **Christ** is to attack Him. Then the question: "Why do you kick against the goads?" The ox goads were sharp spikes implanted in a wooden frame that were fastened to oxcarts behind the oxen. If an ox became stubborn and refused to move forward, it sometimes registered its stubbornness by kicking its feet backward into the goad. Imagine how dumb an ox would be if after once kicking the goad, it became so furious that it kicked it again and again. The more it kicks the goads, the more pain it inflicts on itself. It is like a man banging his head against the wall and finding solace in how good it feels when he stops.

The voice was saying to Saul, "You dumb ox! How stupid it is to keep kicking the goads. You cannot win. Your battle is futile. It is time to surrender." Saul's response was a simple question, but the question was loaded: "Who are you, Lord?" Saul did not know the identity of the One who had just overpowered him, but of one thing he was certain—whoever it was, He was Lord.

In this experience Saul became Paul just as Jacob had become Israel. The battle was over. Saul struggled with God and lost. Here, like Isaiah, Saul received his call, his commission to apostleship. His life was changed, and the course of world history was changed with it. In defeat Paul found peace.

After telling this story to King Agrippa, Paul added these words: "So then, King Agrippa, I was not disobedient to the vision from heaven." As zealous as Saul had been in his fight *against* Christ, he became even more zealous in his fight *for* Christ. He had a vision of God's holiness that was so intense, he never forgot it. He contemplated it and expounded its meaning throughout his epistles. He became a man who understood what it meant to be justified. For him the holy war was over, and he entered into a holy peace. He became the apostle whose writings awakened Luther in the monastery and gave to the Christian church the recipe for an abiding peace with God.

The struggle we have with a holy God is rooted in the conflict between God's righteousness and our unrighteousness. He is just, and we are unjust. This tension creates fear, hostility, and anger within us toward God. The unjust person does not desire the company of a just judge. We become fugitives, fleeing from the presence of One whose glory can blind us and whose justice can condemn us. We are at war with Him unless or until we are justified. Only the justified person can be comfortable in the presence of a holy God.

The apostle Paul sets forth immediate benefits— fruits of justification. In his Epistle to the Romans he explains what happens to us when we are justified, when we are covered by Christ's righteousness, which is by faith: "Therefore, since we have been justified through faith, we have peace with God through our Lord Jesus Christ, through whom we have gained access by faith into this grace in which we now stand. And we rejoice in the hope of the glory of God" (Rom. 5:1-2).

The first fruit of our justification is *peace with God.* To the ancient Jew peace was a precious but elusive commodity. The present-day turmoil in the Middle East seems like a replay of ancient history. From the days of the conquest of Canaan to the period of Roman occupation in New Testament times, there were only a few years when Israel was not at war. The location of Palestine as a pivotal land bridge between Africa and Asia made it a corridor not only for trade but also for warfare. Tiny Israel often found itself caught between competing world powers and was used like a military Ping-Pong ball.

The Jews longed for peace. They yearned for the day when swords would be beaten into plowshares. They waited for the era when the Prince of Peace would come to end the incessant hostilities. So important to the Jews was their quest for peace, that the very word *peace* became a daily greeting. Where we say hello or good-bye, Jews simply said shalom. To this day the greeting *shalom* remains an integral part of Jewish vocabulary.

The word *peace* had its primary reference to the cessation of military conflict. But a deeper meaning was attached to it as well. The Jews were also deeply concerned for inner peace, for the tranquil rest of the soul that meant an end to a troubled spirit. We have a similar concept in view when we speak of "peace of mind."

I remember the sultry summer day in 1945 when I was busy playing stickball in the streets of Chicago. At that time my world consisted of the piece of real estate that extended from one manhole cover to the next. All that was important to me was that my turn at bat had finally come. I was most annoyed when the first pitch was interrupted by an outbreak of chaos and noise all around me. People started running out of apartment doors, screaming and beating dishpans with wooden spoons. I thought for a moment it might

be the end of the world. It was certainly the end of
my stickball game. In the riotous confusion I saw
my mother rushing toward me with tears streaming
down her face. She scooped me up in her arms and
squeezed me, sobbing over and over again, "It's over.
It's over. It's over!"

It was VJ Day, 1945. I wasn't sure what it all meant,
but one thing was clear. It meant that the war had
ended and that my father was coming home. No more
airmail to faraway countries. No more listening to the
daily news reports about battle casualties. No more
silk banners adorned with stars hanging in the window. No more crushing of tin soup cans. No more ra-
tion coupons. The war was over, and peace had come
to us at last.

That moment of jubilation left a lasting impression on my childhood brain. I learned that peace is
an important thing, a cause for unbridled celebration
when it was established and for bitter remorse when
it was lost.

The impression I got that day in the streets of Chicago was that peace had arrived forever. I had no idea
how fragile it was. It seemed like a very short time
before news reporters like Gabriel Heater were giving
ominous warnings about troop buildups in China, the
nuclear threat of Russia, and the blockade of Berlin.
The peace of America was short lived, yielding once
more to warfare in Korea and then again in Vietnam.

Fragile. Unstable. Tenuous. These are the normal
conditions of earthly peace. Peace treaties, like rules,
seem to be made to be broken. A million Neville
Chamberlains leaning over balconies with hands out-

stretched, declaring, "We have achieved peace for our time" would not ensure that human history is ever anything but one continuous Munich.

We soon learn not to trust too heavily in peace. War intrudes too quickly, too easily. Yet we long for a lasting peace that we can depend on. This is precisely the kind of peace the apostle Paul declared in his Epistle to the Romans.

When our holy war with God ceases; when we, like Luther, walk through the doors of paradise, when we are justified by faith, the war ends forever. With the cleansing from sin and the declaration of divine forgiveness we enter into an eternal peace treaty with God. The firstfruit of our justification is peace with God. This peace is a holy peace, a peace unblemished and transcendent. It is a peace that cannot be destroyed.

When God signs a peace treaty, it is signed for perpetuity. The war is over, forever and ever. Of course we still sin; we still rebel; we still commit acts of hostility toward God. But God is not a cobelligerent. He will not be drawn into warfare with us. We have an advocate with the Father. We have a mediator who keeps the peace. He rules over the peace because He is both the Prince of Peace and He is *our* peace.

We are now called the children of God, a title granted in blessing to those who are peacemakers. Our sins are now dealt with by a Father, not a military commander. We have peace. It is our possession, sealed and guaranteed for us by Christ.

Our peace with God is not fragile; it is stable. When we sin, God is displeased, and He will move to correct us and convict us of our sin. But He does not go to war against us. His bow is no longer bent, and the arrows of His wrath are no longer aimed at our hearts. He does not rattle His sword every time we break the treaty.

The peace of justification is not only external. The deepest longings for inward peace are also met in Christ. It was St. Augustine who once prayed, "Thou hast made us for Thyself, and our heart is restless, until it finds its rest in Thee." We all know what it means to be stricken with inner restlessness. We know the gnawing feelings of emptiness and guilt that come from estrangement from God. Once our peace is established, that awful emptiness is filled, and our hearts may be still.

The New Testament calls this peace the peace that passes understanding. It is a holy peace, a peace that is "other" than routine earthly peace. It is the kind of peace that only Christ can bestow. It is the kind of peace that Christ Himself possessed.

We know from the Gospel records that Jesus had few possessions in this world. He owned no home; He had no place to lay His head. He had no business or corporate stocks. His one possession was His robe. That valuable robe was stolen from Him by those appointed to execute Him. It would seem, then, that He died penniless, with no inheritance to bequeath to His heirs.

We are the heirs of Christ. At first glance it would seem that we are heirs without an inheritance. Yet the Bible makes it clear that God has been pleased to give His kingdom to His beloved Son. Jesus had an inheritance from His Father, and that inheritance He has passed on to us. He promised that someday we will hear the words, "Come, you who are blessed by my Father; take your inheritance, the kingdom prepared for you since the creation of the world" (Matt. 25:34).

The kingdom of God is not our only inheritance. In His last will and testament, Jesus left His heirs something else, something very special: "Peace I leave with you; my peace I give you. I do not give to you as the world gives. Do not let your hearts be troubled and do not be afraid" (John 14:27).

This is the legacy of Christ: *peace.* It is His peace that is our inheritance. He gives the gift in a way that is different from gifts that are given in this world. There are no ulterior motives and no sinister strings attached. He gives us His peace not for His benefit but for ours. It is an otherworldly gift given in an otherworldly manner. It is ours to keep forever.

Peace is only one immediate fruit of justification. Added to this holy peace is something else: *access.* The word *access* is crucial to anyone who has ever wrestled with a holy God. We see signs all around us about access. One sign may read, "No Access," and another reads, "Limited Access." At one time in history a "No Access" sign was posted at the gates of Paradise. Even the Old Testament temple allowed ordinary people no access to the throne of God. Even the high priest's access was "limited" to once a year under very guarded circumstances. A thick veil separated the Holy of Holies from the rest of the temple. It was off-limits. Restricted. No admission was permitted to the rank-and-file believer.

The moment Jesus was slain, the instant the Just One died for the unjust, the veil in the temple was torn. The presence of God became accessible to us. For the Christian the "No Access" sign was removed from the gates of paradise. We may now walk freely on holy ground. We have access to His grace, but even more, we have access to Him. Justified people need no longer say to the Holy One, "Depart from me, for I am a sinful man." Now we can feel welcome in the presence of a holy God. We can take our questions to Him. He is not too remote to hear our cries. We come as those covered by the righteousness of Christ. I repeat: *We can feel welcome in the presence of God.* To be sure we still come in awe, in a spirit of reverence and adoration, but the tremendous news is that we can come:

> Therefore, since we have a great high priest who has gone through the heavens, Jesus the Son of God, let us hold firmly to the faith we profess. For we do not have a high priest who is unable to sympathize with our weaknesses, but we have one who has been tempted in every way, just as we are—yet was without sin. Let us then approach the throne of grace with confidence, so that we may receive mercy and find grace to help us in our time of need. (Heb. 4:14-16)

The Bible invites us to approach the throne of grace with confidence. Other translators use the word *boldness.* As justified people we may be bold in approaching God. To be bold or confident must not be confused with being arrogant or flip. Uzzah was more than bold; he was arrogant. Nadab and Abihu went beyond confidence to insulting the majesty of God. We are to come into His presence boldly and in confidence. There is no need to retreat from Him or to hesitate to enter. But when we come, we must remember two things: (1) who He is; and (2) who we are.

For the Christian the holy war is over; the peace has been established. Access to the Father is ours. But we still must tremble before our God. He is still holy. Our trembling is the tremor of awe and veneration, not the trembling of the coward or the pagan frightened by the rustling of a leaf. Luther explained it this way: We are to fear God not with a servile fear like that of a prisoner before his tormentor but as children who do not wish to displease their beloved Father. We come to Him in confidence; we come to Him in boldness; we have access. We have a holy peace.

Allowing God's Holiness to Touch Our Lives

As you reflect about what you have learned and rediscovered about God's holiness, answer these questions. Use a journal to record your responses to God's holiness, or discuss your responses with a friend.

1. Has God ever engaged you in an honest struggle, as He did Jacob? What was the outcome?
2. Have you ever challenged God, as Job did? What was God's response?
3. Habakkuk's battle with God ended in a bold statement of faith: "Even if _____

happens, yet I will rejoice in the Lord."
What are the "even if's" in your life? Are you
willing to surrender them to the Lord?

4. What does it mean to you personally that
Christ's death offers us unending peace with
God?

5. How will you worship God for giving us
unlimited access to Himself?

Be Holy Because I Am Holy

Apollyon, beware what you do;

for I am in the king's highway,

the way of holiness;

Therefore take heed to yourself.

JOHN BUNYAN

Christians in the early church were called saints. Since that time the word *saint* has undergone strong changes in our vocabulary. Now the word *saint* conjures up images of a super-righteous person, a person of extraordinary piety and spiritual power. The Roman Catholic church has made it a title for those who have been canonized into a special list of spiritual heroes and heroines.

The Bible uses the word *saint* for the rank-and-file believer. In the New Testament all of the people of God enjoy the title *saint*. The word means simply "holy one." The New Testament saints were the holy ones. It seems odd that the term is used for believers who were struggling with all sorts of sin. When we read the epistles of Paul, we are struck by the fact that he addresses the people as saints and then goes on to rebuke them for their foolish and sinful behavior.

The saints of Scripture were called saints not because they were already pure but because they were people who were set apart and called to purity. The word *holy* has the same two meanings when applied to people as it has when it is applied to God. We recall that when the word *holy* is used to describe God, it not only calls attention to that sense in which He is different or apart from us, but it also calls attention to His absolute purity. But we are not God; we are not transcendent; we are certainly not pure. How then can the Bible possibly call us "holy ones"?

To answer that question, we must look back to the Old Testament. When God led Israel out of bondage in Egypt and made them a special nation, He set them apart. He called them His chosen people and gave them a special commission. He said to them, "Be holy, because I am holy" (Lev. 11:44).

This special call to Israel was really not new. It did not begin with Moses or even with Abraham. The call to holiness was first given to Adam and Eve. This was the original assignment of the human race. We were created in the image of God. To be God's image meant, among other things, that we were made to mirror and reflect God's character. We were created to shine forth to the world the holiness of God. This was the chief end of man, the very reason for our existence.

Presbyterian churches have made use of the Westminster Catechism in the instruction of children. The first question of the catechism reads: "What is the chief end of man?" The question asks about the primary responsibility carried by every human being. The answer to the question reads: "Man's chief end is to glorify God and to enjoy Him forever."

I had a hard time with that question when I was a boy. I couldn't quite put the two parts of the answer together. I was unable to see how enjoyment fit with glorifying God. I realized that to glorify God involved some kind of obedience to His holy law. That did not sound like much fun. Already I knew the conflict between my own enjoyment and obeying the laws of God. I dutifully recited the required answer even though I had no real understanding of it. I saw God as a barrier to joy. To live to His glory as my chief goal was not what I had in mind. I guess Adam and Eve had a little trouble with it too.

A big problem I had in my youth was that I did not quite understand the difference between happiness and pleasure. I would like to report to you that since I have become a man, I have put away all childish things. Unhappily, that is not the case. There are still childish things that cling to my adult life. I still struggle with the difference between happiness and pleasure. I know the difference in my head, but it has not yet reached my bloodstream.

I have committed many sins in my life. Not one of my sins has ever made me happy. None has ever added a single ounce of happiness to my life. Quite the contrary. Sin has added an abundance of unhappiness to my life. I stand amazed at those famous personalities who, in the course of television or magazine interviews, declare that if they had their lives to live over, they would do nothing differently. Such foolishness staggers my imagination. There are multitudes of things I would love to have the chance to do over. Now it is quite possible that with a second chance, I would make the same foolish mistakes, but I'd still like the chance to try.

My sins have not brought me happiness. But my sins have brought me pleasure. I like pleasure. I am still very much attracted to pleasure. Pleasure can be great fun. And not all pleasures are sins. There is much pleasure to be found in righteousness. But the difference is still there. Sin can be pleasurable, but it never brings happiness.

Now if I understand all this, why would I ever be tempted to sin? It seems silly that anyone who knows the difference between happiness and pleasure would continue to trade happiness for pleasure. It seems utterly stupid for a person to do something that he knows will rob him of his happiness. Yet we do it. The mystery of sin is not only that it is wicked and destructive but also that it is so downright stupid.

I smoked cigarettes for years. I never really kept count, but my guess is that during those years, hundreds of people called my attention to the fact that smoking was not a good thing for me to be doing. They were merely pointing out to me the obvious, telling me what every smoker in America already knows. Before I was ever converted to Christianity, I knew full well that smoking was harmful to me. I knew it before the surgeon general ever put a warning label on cigarette packages. I knew it from the first cigarette I ever smoked. Yet I continued to do it. Sheer madness. That is what sin is.

Have you ever done anything that you felt like doing even though your head told you it was wrong? If you answer no to that question, you are either lying or deluded. We all fall into this trap. We do what we feel like doing rather than what we know we ought to do. No wonder we cry like Paul, "What a wretched man I am! Who will rescue me from this body of death?" (Rom. 7:24).

Our problem is that we have been called to be holy, and we are not holy. Yet again the question arises, If we are not holy, why does the Bible call us saints?

The Bible calls us "holy ones." We are holy because we have been consecrated to God. We have been set apart. We have been called to a life that is different. The Christian life is a life of nonconformity. The idea of nonconformity is expressed in Romans:

> Therefore, I urge you, brothers, in view of God's mercy, to offer your bodies as living sacrifices, holy and pleasing to God—this is your spiritual act of worship. Do not conform any longer to the pattern of this world, but be transformed by the renewing of your mind. Then you will be able to test and approve what God's will is—his good, pleasing and perfect will. (Rom. 12:1-2)

In the Old Testament, worship centered on the altar with the presentations of sacrifices offered to God. For the most part, these sacrifices of animals and various grains were made as sin offerings. In themselves the animal sacrifices had no power to atone for sins. They were symbols that pointed forward to the one great sacrifice that would be made on the cross. After the perfect Lamb was slain, the altar sacrifices ceased. The Christian church has no provision for animal sacrifices anymore because it has no need for such sacrifices. To offer them now would be to insult the perfection of Christ's sacrifice.

Because the days of animal sacrifices are over,

many people assume that all sacrifices offered to God are abhorrent to Him. That is simply not true. Here the apostle Paul calls for a new kind of sacrifice, a *living sacrifice* of our bodies. We are to give to God not our grains or our animals, but ourselves. This new sacrifice is not an act of atonement; it is not a sin offering. The sacrifice of our bodies to God is a thank offering. It follows upon Paul's word *therefore*.

When we see the word *therefore* in the text of Scripture, we are immediately alerted that a conclusion is coming. The word *therefore* links what has been previously said to what is about to be concluded. In Romans 12 the "therefore" refers to all the apostle has stated in the previous chapters regarding Christ's saving work on our behalf. The word drives us forward to the only proper conclusion we can draw from His work. In light of the gracious justification that Christ has achieved for us, the only reasonable conclusion we can reach is that we ought to present ourselves totally to God as walking, breathing, living sacrifices.

What does the living sacrifice look like? Paul first describes it in terms of nonconformity. "Do not conform any longer to the pattern of this world." Here is the point at which many Christians have gone astray. It is clear that we are to be nonconformists. But it is difficult to understand precisely what kind of nonconformity is called for. Nonconformity is a tricky matter and can easily be reduced to superficiality.

It is a tragedy that the matter of nonconformity has been treated by Christians at a shallow level. The simplistic way of not conforming is to see what is in style in our culture and then do the op-

posite. If short hair is in vogue, the nonconformist wears long hair. If going to movies is popular,
then Christians avoid movies as "worldly." The extreme case of this may be seen in groups that refuse to wear buttons or use electricity because such
things, too, are worldly.

A superficial style of nonconformity is the classical
pharisaical trap. The kingdom of God is not about
buttons, movies, or dancing. The concern of God is
not focused on what we eat or what we drink. The
call of nonconformity is a call to a deeper level of
righteousness that goes beyond externals. When piety
is defined exclusively in terms of externals, the whole
point of the apostle's teaching has been lost. Somehow
we have failed to hear Jesus' words that it is not what
goes into a person's mouth that defiles a person, but
what comes out of that mouth. We still want to make
the kingdom a matter of eating and drinking.

Why are such distortions rampant in Christian cir-
cles? The only answer I can give is sin. Our marks of
piety can actually be evidences of impiety. When we
major in minors and blow insignificant trifles out of
proportion, we imitate the Pharisees. When we make
dancing and movies the test of spirituality, we are
guilty of substituting a cheap morality for a genuine
one. We do these things to obscure the deeper issues
of righteousness. Anyone can avoid dancing or going
to movies. These require no great effort of moral
courage. What is difficult is to control the tongue, to
act with integrity, to reveal the fruit of the Spirit.

I have never heard a sermon on coveting. I have
heard plenty of sermons about the evils of whiskey,

but none on the evils of covetousness. Strange. To be sure, the Bible declares that drunkenness is sin, but drunkenness never made the top-ten list. True nonconformists stop coveting; they stop gossiping; they stop slandering; they stop hating and feeling bitter; they start to practice the fruit of the Spirit.

Jesus rebuked the Pharisees for their preoccupation with external matters:

> Woe to you, teachers of the law and Pharisees, you hypocrites! You give a tenth of your spices—mint, dill and cummin. But you have neglected the more important matters of the law—justice, mercy and faithfulness. You should have practiced the latter, without neglecting the former. You blind guides! You strain out a gnat but swallow a camel. (Matt. 23:23-24)

Jesus rebuked the scribes and the Pharisees for neglecting weighty matters and overemphasizing minor matters. He saw this issue not as an *either-or* matter but a *both-and* matter. Tithes were to be paid, but not as a substitute for paying great care to issues of justice, mercy, and fidelity. The Pharisees took care of outward, external, visible matters of piety but ignored the higher spiritual issues.

Anyone can be a nonconformist for nonconformity's sake. Again I want to emphasize that this is a cheap piety. What we are ultimately called to is more than nonconformity; we are called to *transformation*. We notice that the words *conform* and *transform* both contain the same root word *form*. The only difference between the two words is found in the prefixes. The prefix *con* means "with." To conform, then, is to be "with the structures or forms." In our culture a conformist is someone who is "with it." A nonconformist may be regarded as someone who is "out of it." If the goal of the Christian is to be "out of it," then I am afraid we have been all too successful.

The prefix *trans* means "across" or "beyond." When we are called to be transformed, it means that we are to rise above the forms and the structures of this world. We are not to follow the world's lead but to cut across it and rise above it to a higher calling and style. This is a call to transcendent excellence, not a call to sloppy "out-of-it-ness." Christians who give themselves as living sacrifices and offer their worship in this way are people with a high standard of discipline. They are not satisfied with superficial forms of righteousness. The "saints" are called to a rigorous pursuit of the kingdom of God. They are called to depth in their spiritual understanding.

The key method Paul underscores as the means to the transformed life is by the "renewal of the mind." This means nothing more and nothing less than education. Serious education. In-depth education. Disciplined education in the things of God. It calls for a mastery of the Word of God. We need to be people whose lives have changed because our minds have changed.

True transformation comes by gaining a new understanding of God, ourselves, and the world. What we are after ultimately is to be conformed to the image of Christ. We are to be like Jesus, though not in the sense that we can ever gain deity. We are not god-men. But our humanity is to mirror and reflect the perfect humanity of Jesus. A tall order!

To be conformed to Jesus, we must first begin to think as Jesus did. We need the "mind of Christ." We need to value the things He values and despise the things He despises. We need to have the same priorities He has. We need to consider weighty the things that He considers weighty.

That cannot happen without a mastery of His Word. The key to spiritual growth is in-depth Christian education that requires a serious level of sacrifice.

That is the call to excellence we have received. We are not to be like the rest of the world, content to live our lives with a superficial understanding of God. We are to grow dissatisfied with spiritual milk and hunger after spiritual meat.

To be a saint means to be separated. But it means more than that. The saint also is to be involved in a vital process of sanctification. We are to be purified daily in the growing pursuit of holiness. If we are justified, we must also be sanctified.

Luther used a wonderful Latin phrase to describe the status of the justified sinner: *simul justus et peccator.* Let's look at the phrase a word at a time to discern its meaning for us. *Simul* is the Latin word from which our English word *simultaneous* is derived; it means "at one and the same time." *Justus* is the Latin from which our word *just* comes, and *et* is the Latin word for "and." The word *peccator* is probably least familiar to us. We derive the English words *impeccable* and *peccadillo* from it. It is the Latin word for "sinner." Putting the words together, we get *simul justus et peccator*: "at the same time just and sinner." That is what saints are, people who are at one and the same time just, yet sinful.

That saints are still sinners is obvious. How then can they be just? Saints are just because they have been justified. In and of themselves they are not just. They are made just in God's sight by the righteousness of Christ. This is what justification by faith is about. When we put our personal trust for our salvation in Christ and in Him alone, then God transfers to our account all of the righteousness of Jesus. His justness becomes ours when we believe in Him. It is a legal transaction. The transfer of righteousness is like an accounting transaction where no real property is exchanged. That is, God puts Jesus' righteousness in my account while I am still a sinner.

This all sounds something like a fraud, as if God is playing legal games. He counts us righteous even when in and of ourselves we are not righteous. But this is the gospel! This is the Good News, that we can carry an account of perfect righteousness before the judgment throne of a just and holy God. It is the righteousness of Christ that becomes ours by faith. It is no fraud and much less a game. The transaction is real. God's declaration is serious. Christ's righteousness is really put in our account. God sees us as righteous because we have been covered and clothed by the righteousness of Jesus. It is not simply that Jesus pays our debts for us by dying. His life is as important to us as His death. Not only does Christ take our sins, our debts, and our demerits, but He also gives us His obedience, His assets, and His merits. That is the only way an unjust person can ever stand in the presence of a just and holy God.

This concept of a transfer of righteousness is fraught with peril. It is easily confused and seriously abused. Some people assume that if we believe in Christ, we never have to worry about changing our lives. Justification by faith may be viewed as a license to sin. If we have the righteousness of Christ, why should we worry about changing our sinful ways? Since our good works can't get us into heaven, why should we be concerned about them at all? Such questions never ought to pass over the lips of a truly justified person.

When Luther boldly declared the biblical doctrine of justification by faith alone, he said, "Justification is by faith alone, but not by a faith that is alone." James had said it earlier in a different way. He said that "faith without deeds is dead" (James 2:26). True faith, or saving faith, is what Luther called a *fides viva,* a "living faith." It is a faith that immediately brings forth the fruits of repentance and righteousness. If we say we have faith, but no works follow, that is clear evidence that our faith is not genuine. True faith always produces real conformity to Christ. If justification happens to us, then sanctification will surely follow. If there is no sanctification, it means that there never was any justification.

The instant we believe, we are immediately justified. God does not wait for our good works before He declares us just. We are still sinners when the declaration comes.

How much time elapses before the sinner begins to

become pure? The answer is *none*. There is no time lapse between our justification and the *beginning* of our sanctification. But there is a great time lapse between our justification and the *completion* of our sanctification.

Luther used a simple analogy to explain it. He described the condition of a patient who was mortally ill. The doctor proclaimed that he had medicine that would surely cure the man. The instant the medicine was administered, the doctor declared that the patient was well. At that instant the patient was still sick, but as soon as the medicine passed his lips and entered his body, the patient began to get well. So it is with our justification. As soon as we truly believe, at that very instant we start to get better; the process of becoming pure and holy is underway, and its future completion is certain.

The goal of Christian growth is the achievement of righteousness. In the Christian world today such a statement may sound radical. Christians hardly ever talk about righteousness. The word has almost become a swear word. Nearly any other term is preferred to the word *righteousness*. I have never had a student, a parishioner, or any other person come to me and ask, "How can I become righteous?"

Many people have spoken to me about being ethical, moral, spiritual, or even pious. But nobody seems to want to talk about being righteous. Perhaps it is because we know it is a sin to be self-righteous. The word *righteous* sounds a bit pharisaical. It sounds more spiritual to talk about being spiritual than it does to talk about being righteous.

To be spiritual has only one real purpose. It is a means to an end, not the end itself. The goal of all spiritual exercise must be the goal of righteousness. God calls us to be holy. Christ sets the priority of the Christian life: "But seek first his kingdom and his righteousness, and all these things will be given to you as well" (Matt. 6:33). The goal is righteousness.

How can we know if we are moving ahead in our pursuit of righteousness? How can we know if we are making real progress in our call to be holy? The Bible sheds light on these questions. Righteous people are known by their fruit. They become holy by the sanctifying power of the Holy Spirit working in them and on them. The Holy Spirit knows what holiness is. He is called the Holy Spirit not only because He is holy Himself but also because He is working to produce holiness in us.

The fruit of righteousness is that fruit that is exercised in us by the Holy Spirit. If we want to be holy, if we have a real hunger for righteousness, then we must focus our attention on the fruit of the Holy Spirit.

The fruit of the Holy Spirit is set forth for us in stark contrast to the fruit of our sinful nature:

> The acts of the sinful nature are obvious:
> sexual immorality, impurity and debauchery;
> idolatry and witchcraft; hatred, discord,
> jealousy, fits of rage, selfish ambition,
> dissensions, factions and envy; drunkenness,
> orgies, and the like. I warn you, as I did before,
> that those who live like this will not inherit the
> kingdom of God. (Gal. 5:19-21)

In this passage Paul echoes Jesus' warning about the loss of the kingdom of God. People whose lives are characterized by the styles mentioned above will not inherit the kingdom of God. This is not to say that any sin we commit will mean the forfeiture of heaven. Paul is talking about a lifestyle that is habitually and consistently characterized by the vices mentioned. The list includes both external and internal sins, sins of the body and sins of the heart.

The sins listed may be described as gross and heinous sins. The New Testament recognizes degrees of sins. Some sins are worse than others. This important point is often overlooked by Christians. Protestants particularly struggle with the concept of gradations or degrees of sin. This is partly due to a reaction to the Roman Catholic idea of two kinds of sins: mortal and venial. Rome calls certain sins "mortal" because they are so serious that they kill the grace in our soul. Lesser sins are called "venial"; they fall short of destroying saving grace.

We tend to think that sin is sin and that no sin is greater than any other. We think of Jesus' teaching in the Sermon on the Mount that to lust after a woman is to be guilty of adultery. We are aware that the Bible teaches if we sin against one point of the law, we sin against the whole law. These two biblical teachings can easily confuse us about the degrees of sin.

When Jesus said that to lust is to violate the law against adultery, He did not say or imply that lust is *as bad as* the full act of adultery. His point was that the full measure of the law prohibited more than the actual act of adultery. The law has a broader application.

The Pharisees thought that because they never committed the actual act of adultery, they were free of sin against the law. They assumed that if they actually refrained from killing people, they were keeping the law against killing. They failed to see that unjust anger and hatred were also included in the wider meaning of the law against killing.

Jesus taught that hate is a sin against another person's life. Hatred violates people. It is not as severe as actual murder, but it is nevertheless a sin. The smallest sin involves a sin against the whole law. The law is the standard of holiness for us. In our slightest transgression we sin against that standard; we violate the call to holiness. Again, that does not imply that every sin is as wicked as every other sin. Jesus repeatedly spoke of degrees of punishment in hell as well as of those whose guilt was greater than others.

The idea of gradations of sin is important for us to keep in mind so we understand the difference between *sin* and *gross sin*. Again, all of our sins require forgiveness. All of our sins are acts of treason against God. We need a Savior for our "little" sins as well as for the "major" ones. But some sins are more significant than others, and we need to identify which these are, lest we fall into the pharisaical trap of majoring in the minors.

Consider the attention that is given to the problem of being overweight in our society. Each year people in the United States spend billions of dollars on dieting. There are some excellent reasons for us to keep our body weight under control. We know that obesity is a major health problem. We also know that gluttony is a sin. We are prone to stuffing and stretching the temple of the Holy Spirit. But the accent on our national concern for slimness is not so much a focus on health or gluttony as it is a view based on cosmetics. We want to be slim so that we will look nice. There is nothing wrong with that. But slimness is not the highest measure we can find for holiness. No one has ever hurt me because they were overweight. They have hurt me because they slandered me. We spend little money controlling the slander problem. Maybe it is because some things are more difficult to control than weight. Some people have mastered the art of appetite control. No one has mastered the art of tongue control.

Think of the people whom you consider to be the most godly people you've met. How much does their weight enter into the godliness you've admired? How many of these godly people have vicious tongues? It's a contradiction in terms, isn't it? Godliness and an uncontrolled tongue are incompatible.

The fruit of the Spirit stands in vivid contrast to the sins of the flesh. The fruit of the Spirit yields the virtues we recognize in godly people. Consider the fruit Paul mentions: "But the fruit of the Spirit is love, joy, peace, patience, kindness, goodness, faithfulness, gentleness and self-control" (Gal. 5:22-23).

These are the marks of a person who is growing in holiness. These are the virtues we are called to cultivate. To yield the fruit of the Spirit, we must practice the fruit of the Spirit. The Spirit is at work within us to assist us in the practice of the fruit, but we are called to strive with all our might to produce this fruit.

In this list of the fruit of the Spirit, the apostle gives us a recipe for our sanctification. We all like to learn things in ten easy lessons. There is nothing easy about becoming holy. Yet, the Bible does make it easy for us to know what holiness is supposed to look like. The fruit of the Spirit—that is where our focus must be. Paul simplifies it for us. He adds the following words to his list of virtues that comprise the fruit of the Spirit: "Against such things there is no law. Those who belong to Christ Jesus have crucified the sinful nature with its passions and desires. Since we live by the Spirit, let us keep in step with the Spirit. Let us not become conceited, provoking and envying each other" (Gal. 5:23-26).

Allowing God's Holiness to Touch Our Lives

As you reflect about what you have learned and redis-covered about God's holiness, answer these questions. Use a journal to record your responses to God's holi-ness, or discuss your responses with a friend.

1. What does it mean to you to be holy, to live a holy life?
2. How are you trying to renew your mind?
3. How do you respond when you realize that God has justified you by transferring to your account all of Christ's righteousness?
4. What fruit has the Holy Spirit been developing in your life?
5. In what ways do you want to grow in holiness?

CHAPTER NINE

God in the Hands of Angry Sinners

Almost every natural man
that hears of hell, flatters himself
that he shall escape it.

JONATHAN EDWARDS

Perhaps the most famous sermon ever preached in America was Jonathan Edwards's sermon "Sinners in the Hands of an Angry God." Not only has the sermon been reproduced in countless catalogs of preaching, but it is also included in most anthologies of early American literature. So scandalous is this vivid portrayal of unconverted people's precarious state under the threat of hell that some modern analysts have called it utterly sadistic.

Edwards's sermon is filled with graphic images of the fury of divine wrath and the horror of the relentless punishment of the wicked in hell. Such sermons are out of vogue in our age and generally considered in poor taste and based on a pre-enlightened theology. Sermons stressing the fierce wrath of a holy God aimed at impenitent human hearts do not fit with the civic meeting hall atmosphere of the local church. Gone are the Gothic arches; gone are the stained-glass windows; gone are the sermons that stir the soul to moral anguish. Ours is an upbeat generation with the accent on self-improvement and a broad-minded view of sin.

Our thinking goes like this: If there is a God at all,

He is certainly not holy. If He is perchance holy, He is not just. Even if He is both holy and just, we need not fear because His love and mercy override His holy justice. If we can stomach His holy and just character, we can rest in one thing: He cannot possess wrath.

If we think soberly for five seconds, we must see our error. If God is holy at all, if God has an ounce of justice in His character, indeed if God exists as God, how could He possibly be anything else but angry with us? We violate His holiness; we insult His justice; we make light of His grace. These things can hardly please Him.

Edwards understood the nature of God's holiness. He perceived that unholy people have much to fear from such a God. Edwards had little need to justify a scare theology. His consuming need was to preach about God's holiness; to preach it vividly, emphatically, convincingly, and powerfully. He did this not out of a sadistic delight in frightening people but out of compassion. He loved his congregation enough to warn them of the dreadful consequences of facing the wrath of God. He was not concerned with laying a guilt trip on his people but with awakening them to the peril they faced if they remained unconverted.

Let's examine a section of the sermon to get but a taste of its flavor:

> The God that holds you over the pit of
> hell, much as one holds a spider, or some
> loathsome insect, over the fire, abhors you,
> and is dreadfully provoked: his wrath towards
> you burns like fire; he looks upon you as

worthy of nothing else, but to be cast into
the fire; he is of purer eyes than to bear to
have you in his sight; you are ten thousand
times more abominable in his eyes, than the
most hateful venomous serpent is in ours.
You have offended him infinitely more than
ever a stubborn rebel did his prince; and yet,
it is nothing but his hand that holds you from
falling into the fire every moment. It is to be
ascribed to nothing else, that you did not go
to hell the last night; that you were suffered
to awake again in this world, after you closed
your eyes to sleep. And there is no other
reason to be given, why you have not dropped
into hell since you arose in the morning, but
that God's hand has held you up. There is no
other reason to be given why you have not
gone to hell, since you have sat here in the
house of God, provoking his pure eyes by your
sinful wicked manner of attending his solemn
worship. Yea, there is nothing else that is to
be given as a reason why you do not this very
moment drop down into hell.

O sinner! consider the fearful danger you
are in: it is a great furnace of wrath, a wide
and bottomless pit, full of the fire of wrath,
that you are held over in the hand of that
God, whose wrath is provoked and incensed
as much against you, as against many of the
damned in hell. You hang by a slender thread,
with the flames of divine wrath flashing about

it, and ready every moment to singe it, and
burn it asunder; and you have no interest in
any Mediator, and nothing to lay hold of to
save yourself, nothing to keep off the flames of
wrath, nothing of your own, nothing that you
ever have done, nothing that you can do, to
induce God to spare you one moment.[1]

The pace of the sermon is relentless. Edwards
strikes blow after blow to the conscience-stricken
hearts of his congregation. He draws graphic images from the Bible, all designed to warn sinners of
their peril. He tells them that they are walking on
slippery places with the danger of falling from their
own weight. He says that they are walking across the
pit of hell on a wooden bridge supported by rotten
planks that may break at any second. He speaks of
invisible arrows that, like a pestilence, fly at noonday. He warns that God's bow is bent and that the
arrows of His wrath are aimed at their hearts. He
describes God's wrath as great waters rushing against
the floodgates of a dam. If the dam should break, the
sinners would be inundated by a deluge. He reminds
his hearers that there is nothing between them and
hell but air:

Your wickedness makes you as if it were heavy
as lead, and to tend downwards with great
weight and pressure towards hell; and if God
should let you go, you would immediately
sink and swiftly descend and plunge into the
bottomless gulf; and your healthy constitution,

and your own care and prudence, and best
contrivance, and all your righteousness, would
have no more influence to uphold you and
keep you out of hell, than a spider's web would
have to stop a falling rock.[2]

In the application section of the sermon, Edwards
places great stress on the nature and severity of God's
wrath. Central to his thinking is the clear notion that
a holy God must also be a wrathful God. He lists several
key points about God's wrath that we dare not
overlook.

1. *God's wrath is divine.* The wrath of which Edwards
preached was the wrath of an infinite God. He
contrasts God's wrath with human anger or the wrath
of a king for his subject. Human wrath terminates. It
has an ending point. It is limited. God's wrath can go
on forever.

2. *God's wrath is fierce.* The Bible repeatedly likens
God's wrath to a winepress of fierceness. In hell there
is no moderation or mercy given. God's anger is not
mere annoyance or a mild displeasure. It is a consuming
rage against the unrepentant.

3. *God's wrath is everlasting.* There is no end to the
anger of God directed against those in hell. If we had
any compassion for other people, we would wail at
the thought of a single one of them falling into the
pit of hell. We could not stand to hear the cries of
the damned for five seconds. To be exposed to God's
fury for a moment would be more than we could
bear. To contemplate it for eternity is too awful to
consider. With sermons like this we do not want to be

awakened. We long for blissful slumber, for the repose of tranquil sleep.

The tragedy for us is that in spite of the clear warnings of Scripture and of Jesus' sober teaching on this subject, we continue to be at ease about the future punishment of the wicked. If God is to be believed at all, we must face the awful truth that someday His furious wrath will be poured out. Edwards observed:

> Almost every natural man that hears of hell, flatters himself that he shall escape it; he depends upon himself for his own security; he flatters himself in what he has done, in what he is now doing, or what he intends to do. Every one lays out matters in his own mind how he shall avoid damnation, and flatters himself that he contrives well for himself, and that his schemes will not fail.[3]

How do we react to Edwards's sermon? Does it provoke a sense of fear? Does it make us angry? Are we feeling like a multitude of people who have nothing but scorn for any ideas about hell and everlasting punishment? Do we consider the wrath of God as a primitive or obscene concept? Is the very notion of hell an insult to us? If so, it is clear that the God we worship is not a holy God: Indeed He is not God at all. If we despise the justice of God, we are not Christians. We stand in a position that is every bit as precarious as the one that Edwards so graphically described. If we hate the wrath of God, it is because we hate God Himself. We may protest vehemently against these charges, but our vehemence only confirms our hostility toward God. We may say emphatically, "No, it is not God I hate; it is Edwards that I hate. God is altogether sweet to me. My God is a God of love." But a loving God who has no wrath is no God. He is an idol of our own making as much as if we carved Him out of stone.

Jonathan Edwards preached another famous sermon that can be viewed as a sequel of sorts to "Sinners in the Hands of an Angry God." He titled the sermon "Men Naturally God's Enemies." If I can presume to improve Edwards's title, I would suggest instead "God in the Hands of Angry Sinners."

If we are unconverted, one thing is absolutely certain: *We hate God.* The Bible is unambiguous about this point. We are God's enemies. We are inwardly sworn to His ultimate destruction. It is as natural for us to hate God as it is for rain to moisten the earth when it falls. Now our annoyance may turn to outrage. We heartily disavow what I have just written. We are quite willing to acknowledge that we are sinners. We are quick to admit that we do not love God as much as we ought. But who among us will admit to hating God?

Romans 5 teaches clearly: "When we were God's enemies, we were reconciled to him through the death of his Son" (Rom. 5:10). The central motif of the New Testament is the theme of reconciliation. Reconciliation is not necessary for those who love each other. God's love for us is not in doubt. The shadow of doubt hangs over us. It is our love for God that is in question. The natural human mind, what the Bible calls the "carnal mind," is at enmity with God.

We reveal our natural hostility for God by the low esteem we have for Him. We consider Him unworthy of our total devotion. We take no delight in contemplating Him. Even for the Christian, worship is often difficult and prayer a burdensome duty. Our natural tendency is to flee as far as possible from His presence. His Word rebounds from our minds like a basketball from a backboard.

By nature, our attitude toward God is not one of mere indifference. It is a posture of malice. We oppose His government and refuse His rule over us. Our natural hearts are devoid of affection for Him; they are cold, frozen to His holiness. By nature, the love of God is not in us.

As Edwards noted, it is not enough to say that the natural human mind views God as an enemy. We must be more precise. God is our *mortal* enemy. He represents the highest possible threat to our sinful desires. His repugnance to us is absolute, knowing no lesser degrees. No amount of persuasion from philosophers or theologians can induce us to love God. We despise His very existence and would do anything in our power to rid the universe of His holy presence.

If God were to expose His life to our hands, He would not be safe for a second. We would not ignore Him; we would destroy Him. This charge may seem extravagant and irresponsible until we examine once more the record of what happened when God did appear in Christ. Christ was not simply killed. He was murdered by malicious people. The crowds howled for His blood. It was not enough merely to do away with Him, but it had to be done with the accompaniment of scorn and humiliation. We know that His divine nature did not perish on the cross. It was His humanity that was put to death. Had God exposed the divine nature to execution, had He made His divine essence vulnerable to the executioner's nails, then Christ would still be dead and God would be absent from heaven. Had the sword pierced the soul of God, the ultimate revolution would have been successful, and mankind would now be king.

But, we protest, we are Christians. We are lovers of God. We have experienced reconciliation. We have been born of the Spirit and have had the love of God shed abroad in our hearts. We are no longer enemies but friends. All of these things are true for the Christian. But we must be careful, remembering that with our conversion our natural human natures were not annihilated. There remains a vestige of our fallen nature with which we must struggle every day. There still resides a corner of the soul that takes no delight in God. We see its ragged edge in our continued sin, and we can observe it in our lethargic worship. It manifests itself even in our theology.

It has been said that historically three generic types of theology compete for acceptance within the Christian church: Pelagianism, Semi-Pelagianism, and Augustinianism.

Pelagianism is not Christian. It is not merely sub-Christian but strongly anti-Christian. It is basically a theology of unbelief. That it has a stranglehold on many churches is testimony to the power of people's natural enmity toward God. To the Pelagian or liberal there is no supernatural activity. They do not believe in miracles, in Christ's deity, the Atonement, the Resurrection, the Ascension, or the Second Coming. In a word, there is no biblical Christianity to it. It is sheer paganism masquerading as piety.

What of Semi-Pelagianism? It is clearly Christian with its passionate confession of the deity of Christ and its confidence in the Atonement, the Resurrection, and the rest. Semi-Pelagianism is the majority report among evangelical Christians and probably represents the theology of the vast majority of people who read this book. But I am convinced that with all of its virtues, Semi-Pelagianism still represents a theology of compromise with our natural inclinations. It has a glaring defect in its understanding of God. Though it salutes the holiness of God and protests loudly that it believes in God's sovereignty, it still entertains delusions about our ability to incline ourselves to God, to make "decisions" to be born again. It declares that fallen people, who are at enmity with God, can be persuaded to be reconciled even before their sinful hearts are changed. It has people who are not born again seeing a kingdom Christ declared could not be seen and entering a kingdom that cannot be entered without rebirth. Evangelicals today have unconverted sinners who are dead in trespasses and sin bringing themselves to life by *choosing to be born again.* Christ made it clear that dead people cannot choose anything, that the flesh counts for nothing, and that we must be born of the Spirit before we can even see the kingdom of God, let alone enter it. The failure of modern evangelicalism is the failure to understand the holiness of God. If that one point were grasped, there would be no more talk of mortal enemies of Christ coming to Jesus by their own power.

Only Augustinianism sees grace as central to its theology. When we understand the character of God, when we grasp something of His holiness, then we begin to understand the radical character of our sin and helplessness. Helpless sinners can survive only by grace. Our strength is futile in itself; we are spiritually impotent without the assistance of a merciful God. We may dislike giving our attention to God's wrath and justice, but until we incline ourselves to these aspects of God's nature, we will never appreciate what has been wrought for us by grace. Even Edwards's sermon on sinners in God's hands was not designed to stress the flames of hell. The resounding accent falls not on the fiery pit but on the hands of the God who holds us and rescues us from it. The hands of God are gracious hands. They alone have the power to rescue us from certain destruction.

How can we love a holy God? The simplest answer I can give to this vital question is that we can't. Loving a holy God is beyond our moral power. The only kind of God we can love by our sinful nature is an unholy god, an idol made by our own hands. Unless we are born of the Spirit of God, unless God sheds His holy love in our hearts, unless He stoops in His grace to change our hearts, we will not love Him. He is the One who takes the initiative to restore our souls. Without Him we can do nothing of righteousness. Without Him we would be doomed to everlasting alienation from His holiness. We can love Him only because He first loved us. To love a holy God requires grace, grace strong enough to pierce our hardened hearts and awaken our moribund souls.

If we are in Christ, we have been awakened already. We have been raised from spiritual death unto spiritual life. But we still have "sleepers" in our eyes, and at times we walk about like zombies. We retain a certain fear of drawing near to God. We still tremble at the foot of His holy mountain.

Yet as we grow in our knowledge of Him, we gain a deeper love for His purity and sense a deeper dependence on His grace. We learn that He is altogether worthy of our adoration. The fruit of our growing love for Him is the increase of reverence for His name. We love Him now because we see His loveliness. We adore Him now because we see His majesty. We obey Him now because His Holy Spirit dwells within us.

Allowing God's Holiness to Touch Our Lives
As you reflect about what you have learned and rediscovered about God's holiness, answer these questions. Use a journal to record your responses to God's holiness, or discuss your responses with a friend.

1. How do you respond to Jonathan Edwards's sermon? Is it compassionate?
2. How does understanding God's wrath help you honor Him as a holy God?
3. In what ways do you need God to help you love Him?

CHAPTER TEN

Looking beyond Shadows

Truth is always *about* something,
but reality is that *about which* truth is.

C. S. LEWIS

The psalmist was stirred to feelings of awe and reverence as he contemplated the arena in which he lived. As he turned his gaze toward the sky, the realm of the heavens, he was provoked to express his deepest thoughts: "When I consider your heavens, the work of your fingers, the moon and the stars, which you have set in place, what is man that you are mindful of him, the son of man that you care for him? You made him a little lower than the heavenly beings and crowned him with glory and honor" (Ps. 8:3-5).

These were not the sentiments of a professional astronomer or a primitive astrologer. They were the reflections of an ordinary person who was contemplating his small place in a vast universe. The psalmist had no concept of an expanding universe that contained billions of stars and innumerable galaxies. He had no thoughts of exploding novae or of spiral nebulae. He had never heard of Big-Bang cosmology. From his vantage point in space and time, the sky appeared to be a domed canopy whose luminaries were perhaps only a few miles high in the sky.

I wonder what David would have thought if

someone suggested to him that the light from the nearest star (apart from our own sun) took four and a half years to reach planet Earth while traveling at the speed of 186,000 miles per second? It is almost impossible for us to contemplate such distances and spatial enormity, even though we live on this side of the Copernican Revolution. When we consider that our planet is twenty-five thousand miles in circumference and that light can go around the world seven and a half times in a single second, we are reduced to sheer astonishment. That astonishment is compounded almost infinitely when we think of the number of seconds in a day, not to mention the number of seconds in four and a half years. But that measurement is only to the nearest star. We have no meaningful analogies to use to contemplate the distance to the furthest star. Indeed we don't even know what star is the furthest star, because in all likelihood it has not been discovered yet.

With the meager resources the psalmist had when he gazed into the night sky of Palestine, he was overwhelmed by the weighty sense of contrast between the magnificence of the heavens and the relative obscurity and insignificance of his own life. By considering the stars, he was forced to ask the ultimate question about his own existence: "What is man that you are mindful of him?" (Ps. 8:4).

We might expect that his conclusion would have been that he was virtually nothing, an insignificant blip on the radar screen of history or a meaningless speck in a cosmic desert. But such was not his conclusion. He expressed a high view of the significance of life on this planet and of the value and dignity of humanity. He spoke of the crown of glory and honor with which the Creator touched this tiny part of creation.

How was the psalmist able to rise to such optimistic heights? Was it merely a case of delusions of grandeur? Was the psalmist armed with a knowledge that was able to bridge the enormous gap between heaven and earth? Perhaps it was because the psalmist was able to perceive something to which we have become almost completely blind. Perhaps it was because the psalmist could see past the stars and the moon to the One who set them in the heavens in the first place.

In his letter to the Romans, the apostle Paul wrote of the revelation that God makes of Himself in and through nature. He says, "For since the creation of the world God's invisible qualities—his eternal power and divine nature—have been clearly seen, being understood from what has been made, so that men are without excuse" (Rom. 1:20).

What Paul says here is startling. He acknowledges the invisibility of God. Yet he speaks of the invisible things of God as being seen. If something is seen, it is not invisible; if it is invisible, it cannot be seen. Why then does the apostle speak of seeing the invisible? Paul was not speaking nonsense or uttering riddles. What he means is this: What cannot be seen *directly* can be seen *indirectly.* In the realm of theology, what Paul is describing is called *mediate revelation.*

Mediate revelation involves a communication or unveiling that takes place through some medium. We use the term *medium* to refer to a source of communication such as newspapers, radio, and television. We receive the information we call news not by being direct eyewitnesses of the events but by reading about them in the print media, by hearing them on the radio, or by watching them on television. Television is such a powerful medium that we may *think* that we are actual eyewitnesses of the events we see on the screen. As we watch a football game in live time, we may feel that we are actually there at the scene. But, of course, we are not. We are watching transmitted images, or pictures, of the event. The game is "visible" to us only via "tele-vision," a medium of communication.

When we turn our attention to the stars, we are engaged in the use of another medium. To look at a star or the moon is not to look at the face of God. It is to look at the handiwork of God. When we gaze at "The Nightwatch" in the Rijksmuseum in Amsterdam, we are not looking at Rembrandt. We are looking at a painting that came from his hand. That painting tells us something about the man who painted it, but it certainly does not tell us everything about him.

Of course, nature in its fullness is a far greater masterpiece than anything Rembrandt ever created. Nature provides us with a much bigger picture than "The Nightwatch." And it reveals far more of its Creator than a painting ever can of its artist. Paul declares that the medium of nature makes visible the invisible power and deity of God Himself.

Paul makes it clear that everybody sees this manifestation of God's majesty. This revelation gets through to all people so that all people see it clearly. The force of Paul's assertion is that every person who has ever lived knows that there is a God and is aware of His transcendent majesty and holiness. The medium God has selected to reveal Himself universally is so clear and so potent that it leaves no one with an excuse. It is a medium far more powerful and effective for its task than a television broadcast. A Barbara Walters interview with God could not show us as much of God as nature does.

Though all people receive this knowledge of God, they will not all readily acknowledge it. After the apostle wrests all excuses from the people's hands, he declares:

> For although they knew God, they neither
> glorified him as God nor gave thanks to him,
> but their thinking became futile and their
> foolish hearts were darkened. Although they
> claimed to be wise, they became fools and
> exchanged the glory of the immortal God
> for images made to look like mortal man and
> birds and animals and reptiles. (Rom. 1:21-23)

Have you ever met Michael Jordan? How would I answer that question if it were asked of me? I could answer it in two different ways. I could say, "Yes, I've met Michael. I've seen him and talked to him." Or I could say, "No, I've never met the man." Both of these answers are true as far as they go. I have seen Michael Jordan. I've seen him on television. I have spoken to him. I have shouted at him while watching the Bulls play on television. Yet, it is also true that I have never met the man. Usually when we talk like this, we add the qualifier "in person." We understand the difference between the real person and the image of the person.

Paul is saying that the real person of God is really known through the real revelation that takes place in the real realm of nature. But the problem is that in the case of God, we distort our knowledge of Him by replacing Him with an image that we create ourselves. This is the essence of idolatry: replacing the reality with a counterfeit. We distort the truth of God and reshape our understanding of Him according to our own preferences, leaving us with a God who is anything but holy.

Again, it is important to note that Paul does not bring a universal indictment against humanity for the failure to know God. That is not our problem. It is not that we fail to know that God is and who God is; it is that we refuse to *believe* what we know to be true. Here we face a problem that is not an intellectual problem. It is a moral problem. It is the problem of dishonesty.

All idolatry is rooted in this fundamental dishonesty. Paul describes this in terms of an exchange, which is a dishonest exchange: "They exchanged the truth of God for a lie, and worshiped and served created things rather than the Creator—who is forever praised. Amen" (Rom. 1:25).

The dishonest exchange that is in view here is the substitution of the creature for the Creator, an exchange that is dishonest precisely because we know better. The late Carl Sagan spoke of the sense of awe and reverence that he felt when he contemplated the intricacies of the cosmos. But Sagan made it clear that this reverence was not for the Author of the cosmos but for the cosmos itself. Sagan's response to the stars was diametrically opposed to the psalmist's response. The psalmist was moved to worship the God who created nature and reveals Himself through nature, not to worship nature itself. This reflects the essential differences between godliness and paganism. Pagans confuse the creature and the Creator. They attribute the glory that properly belongs to God to the creature.

We remember that Paul sees human sin in people's refusal to honor God as God. This refusal is done even though people know the eternal power and deity of the Creator. This refusal to honor God as God is what I think Paul has in mind when he asserts that people refuse to believe what they know is true about God.

The striking conclusion we reach from the apostle's teaching is that God's holiness is not an obscure or arcane secret that may be discovered only by some spiritually elite group of people. Rather God's holiness is on display daily for everyone to see. Again it is not merely that it is available to be seen for those who earnestly search for it. Rather Paul's point is that God's holiness *is seen*, and it is seen clearly.

Elsewhere the apostle indicates that the knowledge of God that is given through creation is not a knowledge we warmly receive and embrace. Instead it is our nature to abhor this knowledge of God's holiness. It is characteristic of the reprobate mind not to want to retain God in our knowledge. We prefer to change the holy into something less than holy. It is this rejection of God's majesty that leaves us with minds that are darkened. It results in a massive foolishness that has disastrous consequences for our lives. Once we refuse to honor God as God, our whole view of life and the world becomes distorted.

Let's return to Psalm 8. Before the psalmist speaks of his contemplation of the stars and the moon and the heavens, he utters a poignant doxology: "O LORD, our Lord, how majestic is your name in all the earth! You have set your glory above the heavens" (Ps. 8:1).

The crucial point that is affirmed by the psalmist is that God's glory is *above the heavens.* The glory of God transcends all creaturely glory. Indeed what glory may be found in this world is borrowed or derived from the Creator's hand. The psalmist is obviously a regenerate man. The psalmist is pleased to honor God as God and to acknowledge the truth of the revelation given in nature. He lifts his eyes above and beyond the splendor of the heavens and rejoices in the glory that is revealed through them.

In his work *The Republic,* Plato uses an illustration that has become famous. Plato tells of men who are chained in the dark interior of a cave. They receive warmth and light from a small fire. All that the men can observe are the flickering shadows cast on the wall of the cave by the fire. This is the extent of their vision. All the reality that they know is that of the shadows. It is not until they are liberated from the confines of the darkness and emerge into the light of day that they can perceive reality as it is. In the meantime, they confuse the shadows on the wall with the real truth.

Plato's analogy was designed to illustrate the difference between what he called *knowledge* and *opinion*. Opinion rests on assumptions drawn from shadows. It fails to penetrate truth. For Plato all knowledge that rests solely on observations of this external world is not true knowledge, but a mere shadow of the truth. To get to the truth, one must get beyond the immediate realm of sense perception to the eternal realm of ultimate reality. He sought to go beyond the phenomena to the ultimate truth and reality.

Though Plato's analogy was written centuries ago, it may be a fitting commentary of the spirit of our own age. We pride ourselves in modern science's explosion of knowledge of the external world. The expansion of the scope of our knowledge has moved well beyond the limits imposed by our naked powers of perception. We probe the realm of the infinitesimal by means of the microscope and the realm of the distant by means of the telescope. Our vision of the near and of the distant now far exceeds what was reached by previous explorations.

Our view of the world around us and the world above us has been so greatly enhanced that it would seem that we have been catapulted into a majestic theater that gives daily displays of remarkable glory. Yet our view of the world is perhaps more earthbound and nearsighted than ever before. Ours is the age of myopia, an age in which we declare that the sum total of reality is the here and now. This is an unprecedented kind of secularism. In our quest for liberation from the sacred and creaturely independence, we have succeeded only in cutting ourselves off from the sacred. We live in a smaller cave than Plato envisioned, and the shadows we behold are cast not by a roaring fire but by rapidly cooling, smoldering embers.

In his *Institutes of the Christian Religion,* sixteenth-century theologian John Calvin offered another analogy, that of the blindfold. He argued that nature is a massive theater, indeed a glorious theater of divine revelation. But we walk through this theater as if we were wearing blindfolds. Calvin's point was not to deny that we actually receive knowledge from natural revelation. Rather he was speaking of the state of people who willfully refuse to turn their gaze to the obvious. We put the blindfolds on ourselves, and then we stumble along, cursing the darkness. The analogy is one designed to underscore human folly, which prefers darkness to light and creatures to the Creator.

Calvin remarks:

> But as the greater part of mankind, enslaved by error, walk blindfold in this glorious theater, he exclaims that it is a rare and singular wisdom to meditate carefully on these works of God, which many, who seem sharp-sighted in other respects, behold without profit. It is indeed true that the brightest manifestation of divine glory finds not one genuine spectator among a hundred. Still neither his power nor his wisdom is shrouded in darkness.[1]

We are creatures who prefer life in the cave to the full light of the blazing sun. The glory of God is all around us. We cannot miss it. However, we not only fail to stop and smell the flowers, but we also fail to notice the glory of the flowers' Maker.

Indeed the featured presentation in the theater of divine majesty in which we walk daily is God's glory. The psalmist declares that the sky and all of nature sing out God's glory and majesty.

We see the inseparable link between God's holiness and His glory. His glory is the outward manifestation of His most perfect being. It is His heaviness or weightiness that is displayed. The Scripture frequently speaks of the cloud of God's glory that at times is made outwardly visible. It is the *shekinah*. This glory cloud overshadowed the disciples on the Mount of Transfiguration. It served as the escort for Jesus in His ascension into heaven and will bear Him when He returns. This glory cloud is so dazzling that it can effect blindness in those who look at it directly, as the apostle Paul did on the road to Damascus.

When God's glory erupted in its full measure in biblical times, the result was terror in all who beheld it. But this cloud of glory is not the only manifestation of God's presence in the Bible. He appeared also in various theophanies such as the burning bush, the pillar of fire, and the tongues of fire that fell at Pentecost. To a lesser degree His glory is manifest everywhere at all times. It can no more be extinguished than can the light of the sun. The sun may be obscured by cloud cover or even undergo periodic eclipses, but such phenomena do not utterly quench its light.

Calvin used the metaphor of "spectacles" or "eyeglasses" to describe our perception of God's glory. He spoke of the spectacles of faith by which believers look beyond the surface of things to feast their eyes on the glory that is plainly there.

The Bible speaks of those who have eyes to see and ears to hear. This reference is not to the ordinary power of the senses but of the ability to cut through the darkness and cacophony of sin to see and hear the truth. With regeneration, the scales fall from our eyes so that we can truly perceive what we see and truly understand what we hear (Mark 4:12). This capacity grows as we mature in our faith.

A few years ago I took up sketching and oil painting as a pastime. My amateur work will never adorn the walls of serious art galleries. I stumble along with this hobby, learning through trial and error. In my earliest instruction, I was told to look at the world around me in a different way. I was taught to pay attention to nuances of shade and shadow, to observe color and texture. Before this exercise, when I passed trees along the road, I saw only trees. Now when I look at trees, I notice the peculiar texture of the bark and the colors highlighted in the leaves. These nuances were always there. I just never noticed them before. Each of these nuances has its own medium to announce the presence of God's glory.

When we are engaged with painting and other art forms, we are interested in beauty. The very concept of beauty is profoundly difficult to define. It is elusive and controversial. The discipline of philosophy has its own subcategory of aesthetics, which seeks to determine norms for beauty. Historically there have been many competing schools of aesthetic thought.

Many people have concluded that there are no rules for beauty, that it is purely a subjective matter. Others, dating back to Aristotle and beyond, have argued for objective criteria for beauty. The subjectivists find refuge in the slogan that "beauty is in the eye of the beholder." This tends to reduce beauty to personal taste or preference, such as found in the various flavors of ice cream. Here one person's beauty is another person's ugliness.

On the other hand some schools of thought have tried to find objective norms by which to judge beauty. Thinkers like Aristotle, Aquinas, and Edwards, for example, have seen beauty based in matters of proportionality, symmetry, complexity, harmony, and the like. The intricate symmetry of complex parts points to elements of beauty. Though it is admitted that the simple may be beautiful, it is more often the harmonic composition of complex parts that points to beauty. We understand the difference between the presentation of stick figures and the structure of the human figure depicted in Michelangelo's work. Likewise, we note the difference between a child playing "Twinkle, Twinkle, Little Star" with one finger and a concert pianist playing Beethoven's *Piano Concerto no. 4*.

What emerges in great art and great music is a depth of dimension that does not quickly become stale or trite. Think, for example, of the difference between Bach's "Jesu, Joy of Man's Desiring" and a current popular song or movie theme. Some popular songs endure for years, but most are short-lived. If, for example, you sat and listened to a popular song for six hours straight, chances are you would become bored with it. Yet if you were to listen intently and continuously to a Bach masterpiece, the piece tends to become more and more fascinating as you discover more intricate nuances to it.

Sometimes people think I am strange when I mention the beauty of professional football games. How could something so primal and violent be said to contain any beauty in it? What I enjoy is watching superbly conditioned athletes who have reached the apex of their sport working together to execute a single movement. Eleven men on one side of the ball each have a specific function to perform in a single play designed to advance the ball only a few feet, while another eleven men on the other side of the ball work together as a unit to prevent that progress. The execution of a play involves a kind of orchestration that requires harmony rather than dissonance. When the harmony is lost, the ball is fumbled or the play is otherwise thwarted.

In all of this, be it art or sport, is revealed a kind of beauty that has profound theological implications. The Old Testament frequently refers to the beauty of God's holiness. Even the garments God designed for Aaron and the priests were designed "for glory and for beauty" (Exod. 28:2, NASB). These references indicate a significant relationship between the holy and the beautiful. We are accustomed to thinking in terms of an inherent relationship between goodness and holiness and between truth and holiness. But truth and goodness are merely two legs of a three-legged stool. The third leg is the element of beauty.

In biblical categories, there is a triad of virtues, all of which point beyond themselves to the holiness of God. This triad is composed of the *good*, the *true*, and the *beautiful*. Let's explore each one.

The ancient philosophers such as Plato and Aristotle sought for what they called the *summum bonum*, or the "highest good." It was this quest that drove them to postulate the existence of God. In their own way, they were attesting what is basic to biblical faith, that the highest good is found in God Himself. He is the norm of norms, and He is without norm. All good finds its root in Him and in His character. He is the fountain of all that is good, and all that is good, in turn, points back to Him. It is only when God is banished from human thought that an ethic of relativism is embraced. But relativism is not so much an ethic as it is an antiethic, which forms the basis of godlessness. It was Dostoyevsky who declared that "If there is no God, then all things are permissible." He understood that without the highest good, there can be no good at all. All "goods" are measured against the ultimate standard of God's goodness.

Just as all goodness finds its definition in the ground of God's goodness, so all truth is judged according to the standard of the truth of God. He is the supreme Author of truth. All that is true not only flows from Him, but it also reflects His character. The ancient theologians understood that all truth is God's truth and that all truth "meets at the top." What is meant by this expression is that no truth is independent of God or contradicts what He declares to be true. Philosophers have offered various theories of truth. One of the most persistent is the so-called *correspondence theory of truth.* This concept defines truth as that which corresponds to reality. The problem with this naked definition is that people have different perceptions of what is true. So the argument ensues: "Truth as perceived by whom?" To transcend this difficulty, we must add to the basic definition the words "as perceived by God." With this addition, the full definition becomes "Truth is that which corresponds to reality as perceived by God." God's perception of truth is perfect. He sees all things from the perspective of eternity. He knows the structure of all reality, both big and small. What He reveals in the Bible is always consistent with His self-revelation in nature. What we learn from the study of nature must square with what we learn from the study of grace. Both spheres belong to God. God is not the author of confusion. He is incapable of speaking lies or contradictions. This is what is meant by the idea that all truth meets at the top. It is not that somehow God can reconcile real contradictions but that no real contradictions infect the clarity of His truth. God's truth is holy truth. That is, His truth expresses His own character. Insofar as He is the fountainhead of all truth, all truth points back to Him. Since all truth points to Him, all truth is sacred. The sacredness of truth is what makes the lie so diabolical in that it distorts our perception of the very character of God.

Just as truth and goodness are rooted in God's character, so is beauty. God Himself is the ground of all unity and diversity, of simplicity and complexity. His very being is internally consistent and harmonious and proportionate. In Him there are no distortions, no disorder, no ugliness. His voice admits to no noise or cacophony. The works of His hands are cosmos, not chaos. Chaos is marked by disorder and confusion; it is manifest irrationally. The beauty of God is a sane and rational beauty in that His being is one of perfect sanity and order. Insofar as the beautiful bears witness to these qualities, they bear witness to Him. Edgar Allan Poe understood that in beauty one encounters the dimension of the sublime, a dimension that is not irrational but may be transrational. That is, beauty, though it involves the mind, goes beyond the limits of mere cognition. When we are "moved" by great works of art, we are gripped by an affective sense that stirs the soul as well as the mind. To cultivate an appreciation for beauty is to set our course to follow after the sublime Author of all beauty.

Medieval theologians used the Latin phrase *ens perfectissimus* to refer to God. The phrase may be translated by the words "the most perfect being." Here the theologians used an expression that is a bit misleading. To say that something or someone is the most perfect being involves a redundancy. Real perfection does not admit to degrees. Something that is truly perfect in every respect cannot become more perfect or most perfect. We speak like this because we are accustomed to dealing with things that are imperfect. Imperfect things can be improved, but the perfect cannot. It should suffice us to say of God simply that He is perfect. Why then did the theologians use the superlative degree to speak of God's perfection? The answer must be found in their desire to underscore the reality of God's perfection so clearly that they would eliminate any possibility of suggesting the slightest lack of perfection in God's character. It was a legitimate use of hyperbole to speak of most perfect.

God's perfection applies to all of His attributes. His power is perfect; it has no weaknesses or any possibility of weakness. His knowledge is not only omniscient but reflects perfect omniscience. There is nothing that God does not know or that He could possibly learn. Some modern theologians have tried to declare that God is omniscient but that His omniscience is a limited omniscience. They assert that God knows everything He can possibly know, but He does not and cannot know certain things, especially the future decisions of free agents. But a limited omniscience is simply not omniscience. And it is not perfect. This view of limited omniscience robs God of His holy omniscience, which is a perfect omniscience. God's love, His wrath, His mercy—all that He is—is perfect. Not only is He perfect, but He is eternally and immutably so. There never was a time when God was less than perfect, and there is no possibility that in the future He may slip into any kind of imperfection. What has been with God will be so forever. His perfection is immutable. It cannot change.

Shadows in a cave are given to change. They dance and flicker with ever-changing shape and brightness. To contemplate the truly holy and to go beyond the surface of creaturely things, we need to get out of our self-made cave and walk in the glorious light of God's holiness.

Allowing God's Holiness to Touch Our Lives

As you reflect about what you have learned and rediscovered about God's holiness, answer these questions. Use a journal to record your responses to God's holiness, or discuss your responses with a friend.

1. Describe a recent experience in which God revealed Himself to you through nature.
2. In what ways do we worship creation rather than the Creator?
3. How do things that are good, true, and beautiful reflect God's holiness? How does this truth help shape your priorities?
4. How will you worship God for His holiness?

CHAPTER ELEVEN

Holy Space and Holy Time

Where, except in the present,
can the Eternal be met?

C. S. LEWIS

N*o Exit.* This famous play written by the French existentialist philosopher Jean Paul Sartre depicts his view that hell is other people, a realm from which there is no exit. The same title may be used to describe our contemporary culture's view of our world. We are a generation of people who feel trapped in the here and now. We sense no access to the heavenly or to the realm of the transcendent. There seems to be an unbridgeable chasm that cuts us off from the arena of the holy. We are doomed, it seems, to live out our days chained to the profane.

As I write these words, a spacecraft is hurtling toward outer space. The astronauts on board are traveling to make repairs and enhancements for the Hubble telescope, which is transmitting to earth unprecedented views of the outer reaches of the universe. As a result, astronomers scramble for new adjustments in their paradigms of cosmology. A myriad of new data impose their presence on us, screaming for explanation. Few scientists still hold to the antiquated view of a steady-state universe, a theory that is being pushed aside by evidence that our universe is ever expanding.

The eighteenth century saw the appearance of a new religion called Deism, which represented a compromise between classical Christian theism and atheistic naturalism. The favorite metaphor of Deism was that of the Divine Clockmaker. God was viewed as the First Cause, who created the world just as a clockmaker designs and constructs a clock. Deists envisioned that just as the clockmaker fits together the springs and gears and then winds up the clock so that it can run on its own inherent power, so God, the great Designer and Maker of the universe, created the world and then stepped back to let the world run by its own mechanical laws. They believe that God made the world a closed system and that He remains eternally aloof from its operation. The Deists see no daily providence, no sacred intrusions from above, and no real possibility of meaningful communication from below.

Deism did not last long as a viable religion. It was not satisfying to either the classical theist or the hard-boiled naturalist. So it quickly passed from the scene. Its abiding significance, however, may be seen in at least two important ways. The first is that, though Deism represented a tiny blip on the radar scope of history, the blip occurred at precisely the time when the United States of America was in its formative stages. Deism was in vogue during the drafting of the Declaration of Independence and the Constitution, and to some degree even traditional Christians at that time accepted Deism's view of natural law.

The second point of Deism's impact was that it favored a view of a closed mechanistic universe that left no room for divine intrusion. Although the religion of Deism is long since past, its view of the world remains current. Many people in our culture think of the world as one that operates by fixed natural laws that function in a manner similar to a winding clock. All causes for all events are rooted strictly in nature, and God is left with nothing to do but to abide as a remote and distant spectator of human events. In our society, religion is limited to a kind of personal therapy for people who have difficulty dealing with the difficulties of life. Ours is a profane existence, with no sense of the presence of the holy.

But people have always looked for a window or door to the transcendent. We seek a threshold that will lead us over the border from the profane to the sacred. It is a quest for sacred space, for ground that is holy ground. Mircea Eliade, one of the leading historians of religion of the twentieth century, has written of this human quest in his book *The Sacred and the Profane*. Eliade insists that we have never been able to create an existence of pure and utter profanity. He says, "To whatever degree he may have desacralized the world, the man who has made his choice in favor of a profane life never succeeds in completely doing away with religious behavior."[1] Humanity seems to be incurably *homo religiosis*. Even within the confines of a closed universe, people seek some place that will serve as a point of access to the transcendent. We feel an aching void that screams to be filled by the holy. We long for holy space.

In Moses' encounter with God in the wilderness, he experienced a threshold to holy space:

Now Moses was tending the flock of Jethro his father-in-law, the priest of Midian, and he led the flock to the far side of the desert and came to Horeb, the mountain of God. There the angel of the LORD appeared to him in flames of fire from within a bush. Moses saw that though the bush was on fire it did not burn up. So Moses thought, "I will go over and see this strange sight—why the bush does not burn up."

When the LORD saw that he had gone over to look, God called to him from within the bush, "Moses! Moses!"

And Moses said, "Here I am."

"Do not come any closer," God said. "Take off your sandals, for the place where you are standing is holy ground." Then he said, "I am the God of your father, the God of Abraham, the God of Isaac and the God of Jacob." At this, Moses hid his face, because he was afraid to look at God. (Exod. 3:1-6)

In this experience of theophany, God commanded Moses to keep himself a safe distance from God's immediate presence. Moses was forbidden to come too close. Then God commanded him to remove his sandals. We have seen in our discussion of the prophet Isaiah's vision that there is a link between the covering of the seraphim's feet and the uncovering of Moses' feet in this event. In both cases the feet point to the condition of creatureliness. In any case Moses was told to remove his sandals because he was standing on holy ground. Moses had entered into holy space. At some point in his walk toward the burning bush, he had crossed a border marking the line between the sacred and the profane. Being a fallen creature of this world, Moses himself was profane. Yet here he dared to walk on earth that was now holy.

The holy space Moses occupied was made holy by God's presence. The composition of the earth at this spot was no different from the earth on the rest of the desert floor. The sacred character of this spot was not intrinsic but extrinsic. That is, it was *made* sacred by a super-added presence. The event that occurred there loaned an extraordinary dimension to the ordinary. The common space had become uncommon by virtue of God's appearance at that spot.

What Moses experienced at the burning bush was not only a theophany but also a hierophany. Just as the word *theophany* refers to a visible manifestation of God, the term *hierophany* refers to an outward manifestation of the holy. Eliade comments, "Every sacred space implies a hierophany, an irruption of the sacred that results in detaching a territory from the surrounding cosmic milieu and making it qualitatively different."[2]

We see a second biblical example of holy space in the account of Jacob's experience at Bethel. In commenting on this Old Testament story, the historian Eliade notes:

> When Jacob in his dream at Haran saw a ladder reaching to heaven, with angels ascending

and descending on it, and heard the LORD speaking from above it, saying: "I am the Lord God of Abraham," he awoke and was afraid and cried out: "How dreadful is this place: this is none other but the house of God, and this is the gate of heaven." And he took the stone that had been his pillow, and set it up as a monument, and poured oil on the top of it. He called the place Beth-el, that is, house of God (Genesis 28:12-19). The symbolism implicit in the expression "gate of heaven" is rich and complex; the theophany that occurs in a place consecrates it by the very fact that it makes it open above—that is, in communication with heaven, the paradoxical point of passage from one mode of being to another.[3]

Several significant images are connected in the interplay of this event. The first is the image of the ladder with the ascending and descending angels. Again we see that the ladder serves as a connecting link between heaven and earth, the sacred and the profane. The ladder describes a way out of the seemingly closed universe. Second, this holy space receives a new name, *Beth-el*, precisely because it is deemed not only the "house of God" but also, perhaps even more important, a virtual gateway. The house does not merely have a portal, it *is* a portal, a door that provides access to heaven.

The third significant dimension of imagery (and I choose the word *significant* for its literal value of that which is "sign bearing") is the image of the stone.

Originally the stone was a common piece of rock used for a common purpose in antiquity, namely to serve as a pillow for Jacob's head as he slept during the night. After the hierophany, the stone is assigned a different purpose. It is transformed from its common purpose to an uncommon purpose. It is anointed with oil in a simple rite of consecration so that it may become a sacred mark for sacred space. It marks what Eliade calls a place of passage between heaven and earth.

Sacred space in biblical times is frequently marked as a place of passage. We see this in the account of Noah and his family as they survive the Deluge:

> By the twenty-seventh day of the second month the earth was completely dry.
>
> Then God said to Noah, "Come out of the ark, you and your wife and your sons and their wives. Bring out every kind of living creature that is with you—the birds, the animals, and all the creatures that move along the ground—so they can multiply on the earth and be fruitful and increase in number upon it."
>
> So Noah came out, together with his sons and his wife and his sons' wives. All the animals and all the creatures that move along the ground and all the birds—everything that moves on the earth—came out of the ark, one kind after another.
>
> Then Noah built an altar to the LORD and, taking some of all the clean animals and

clean birds, he sacrificed burnt offerings on it. (Gen. 8:14-20)

As soon as the waters receded and Noah and his family were able to leave the ark, they built an altar. The immediate purpose for the altar was to provide a platform for making an offering to God. But that was not the only function of the altar. The altar also served to mark the spot of a new beginning, to delineate the place where the passage from destruction to redemption had taken place.

We see similar episodes sprinkled throughout the Old Testament:

> The LORD appeared to Abram and said, "To your offspring I will give this land." So he built an altar there to the LORD, who had appeared to him.

> From there he went on toward the hills east of Bethel and pitched his tent, with Bethel on the west and Ai on the east. There he built an altar to the LORD and called on the name of the LORD. (Gen. 12:7-8)

> From there he went up to Beersheba. That night the LORD appeared to him and said, "I am the God of your father Abraham. Do not be afraid, for I am with you; I will bless you and will increase the number of your descendants for the sake of my servant Abraham."

> Isaac built an altar there and called on
> the name of the LORD. There he pitched
> his tent, and there his servants dug a well.
> (Gen. 26:23-25)

> When Moses went and told the people all the
> LORD's words and laws, they responded with
> one voice, "Everything the LORD has said we
> will do." Moses then wrote down everything
> the LORD had said.

> He got up early the next morning and built an
> altar at the foot of the mountain and set up
> twelve stone pillars representing the twelve
> tribes of Israel. (Exod. 24:3-4)

These passages illustrate instances in which an altar marks sacred space, a crucial passage. Each passage demonstrates a bridge from the merely profane to the holy, either through God's appearance to people or through significant decisions that set the people apart as holy.

Our contact with the holy is not merely an encounter with a different dimension of reality; it is the meeting with Absolute Reality. Christianity is not about involvement with religious experience as a tangent. It involves a meeting with a holy God, who forms the center, or core, of human existence. The Christian faith is theocentric. God is not at the edge of Christians' lives but at the very center. God defines our entire life and worldview.

In our contemporary experience, we experience

holy space in church sanctuaries. The biblical word *church* refers to people, not buildings. Yet when people gather for worship, they need a physical place of meeting. Because the church building is the place designed for worship, we have come to abbreviate the term *church building* as simply *church*. In this sense, churches are designed and built to serve as a kind of sacred space reserved for a place of encounter with the holy.

Church architecture varies. Every church building communicates some kind of nonverbal message. In the past, the Gothic cathedral was designed to focus attention on God's transcendence. The use of high ceilings, vaulted space, towers, and spires all served to communicate that in this building, people met with the holy. While some contemporary church buildings still use spires and vaulted ceilings to suggest God's awesome holiness, other church buildings have been designed to create a fellowship facility. These churches can look more like town meeting halls or even theaters. In some of these churches, the sanctuary becomes a stage, and the congregation becomes an audience. The trend may be seen as a profanation of sacred space to remove any discomfort suggested by the presence and the terror of our holy God. In these settings people are comfortable with other people as they enjoy fellowship with one another.

What is often lost in these functional church designs is the profound sense of *threshold*. A threshold is a place of transition. It signals a change from one realm to another. A friend recently told me of a threshold experience she and her family had. While staying with a relative in St. Louis, my friend, her husband, and two children visited the St. Louis cathedral. As the family walked from the parking lot to the front of the cathedral, they joked and chatted about the warm weather, the emerging daffodils, and other ordinary things. Once they stepped out of the sunlight into the cathedral, the talking abruptly stopped. They were stunned into silence by the magnificent mosaic work that arched high above them in the cathedral's foyer. My friend was especially intrigued by the behavior of her daughter, who had never before been in a cathedral. The teenager started to tiptoe around, as if the sound of her footsteps or the mere touch of her shoes on the floor would disturb something. As the mother and daughter walked into the sanctuary, where 43 million mosaic tiles in over eight thousand shades of color depicted stories from the Bible and from the life of St. Louis, the daughter emitted groans of awe as she stood for ten minutes looking up at the arched ceiling. She then sat in one of the pews, slowly pivoting her head to take in the walls around her. All the while, this normally talkative teenager said nothing. She was overcome by the beauty, the stillness, the holy space. Wanting to explore the transepts and chapels that lined the front of the cathedral, the daughter left the pew and set out to get a closer look. But after having gone only a few steps, she returned to the pew to ask her mother, "Is it all right for me to walk over there?" The mother explained where it was acceptable for her to walk and what places were off-limits.

As my friend watched her daughter explore the rest of the cathedral, the mother realized that without having been told, this teenager had sensed that she was in a holy space. She had crossed a threshold. Also, without having discussed it, this teenager sensed that she, in her humanity, was profane. The sound of her voice, the sound of her footsteps, the touch of her shoes on the floor was somehow offensive to the holiness revealed in this place. She was on holy ground.

It can be argued that such threshold thinking obscures the biblical truth that God is omnipresent and that all of creation is sacred as the theater of God's operations. But the Bible is much more positive about the idea of space. The consecration of sacred space does not end with the close of the Old Testament. It is rooted and grounded in the act of creation itself, and something profoundly important to the human spirit is lost when it is neglected.

Each of our lives is marked by sacred sites that we cherish in our memories. I have an uncanny sense of respect for the room in which I was converted to Christ. I am well aware that the room holds no special power and that it was not the room that converted me. Yet it was *the place* where I first met Christ. This sacred space will always remain as a special place in my life.

In 1996, I led a tour of the sites that were significant to the life of Martin Luther. I visited the Wittenburg church on whose door Luther had tacked his Ninety-five Theses. I was in Erfurt, where he was ordained, and in the Wartburg Castle, where he translated the Bible. Christian history was made in these places. They have a certain sacred significance for me. I had similar feelings when I visited Calvin's church in Geneva and Knox's church in Scotland. Yet these all pale in significance when compared with a journey to the Holy Land. There I felt the place was almost haunted as we stood on the Mount of Olives or walked on the Via Dolorosa. Pilgrims from all over the world have a common sense of the extraordinary when they enter places made sacred by the visitation of God Incarnate. These sites are holy because they were touched by His presence.

God's holiness touches not only space but also time. The Greek language of the New Testament has two different words that can be translated *time*. The first is *chronos*, which usually refers to the ordinary moment-by-moment passing of time. Words like *chronicle*, *chronology*, and *chronometer* all are derived from this Greek word. The second Greek word for time is *kairos*. Kairos refers to special moments that have particular significance. We lack a precise word to translate it into English. The closest we come is the word *historic*. We recognize that all historic events are also historical events, but not all historical events are historic ones. Any event that takes place in history is *historical*. Yet we reserve the term *historic* for events of peculiar importance. Historic events are pivotal moments that shape history from that point on.

In biblical history, kairotic events take place within the context of chronos. Christianity is not a religion that is based simply on vertical events that are wrested out of the context of history. The biblical faith is rooted and grounded within the plane of real history. Though the Bible reveals a special kind of history the scholars call *redemptive* history, it is nevertheless committed to the idea that the redemption that is revealed is revealed in redemptive *history*.

Kairotic events include such crucial moments as the Creation, the Fall, the Exodus, the Captivity, the Incarnation, the Cross, the Resurrection, the Ascension, and Pentecost. These events are watershed moments in God's work in history. They are filled with redemptive significance.

Such kairotic events are often marked in the Bible with the elements of sacred time. These times indicate extraordinary moments of interruptions or intrusions into this world by the holy. In our culture we have the custom of marking certain days with the designation *holiday*, which is an abbreviation for the phrase "holy day." Not every holiday celebrated in our country carries religious connotations with it. Most holidays signify little interest in the holiness of God. Yet because they are deemed particularly important as focal points of remembrance, they are "set apart" from the common or ordinary days of the calendar year.

We are familiar with cultural "rites of passage" that mark off transitional moments in our own lives. These rites are not always linked to religious occasions. In fact, some of the rites may be profane or linked to mythology. But the rites are deemed important precisely because they mark a threshold or moment of transition from one stage or status to another. The popular ballad "Graduation Day" glorified experiences of New Year's Eve, football victories, and the like as being "moments to remember." We mark such times of passage with celebrations, feasts, greeting cards, and other cultural symbols.

The Christian faith includes a significant dimension of sacred time. Sacred time, however, is rooted in real history, not mythology. The first account of sacred time is accomplished by God Himself in His work of creation: "Thus the heavens and the earth were completed in all their vast array. By the seventh day God had finished the work he had been doing; so on the seventh day he rested from all his work. And God blessed the seventh day and made it holy, because on it he rested from all the work of creating that he had done" (Gen. 2:1-3).

God set apart the seventh day as sacred time. When God handed down the Ten Commandments at Mount Sinai, He again announced this seventh day, the Sabbath, as holy, a sacred time that would be integral to the life and faith of Israel. In Christian history the sacred time of the Sabbath has three distinct orientations. The first is the commemoration of God's work of creation. The second is the celebration of God's work of redemption. The third is the celebration of the future promise of the consummation of redemption when we enter our Sabbath rest in heaven. Thus the whole scope of redemptive history, from start to finish, is made sacred in the observance of the Sabbath.

Even profane people try to break out of the monotony of the daily rhythm of time. They seek respite from the weariness of labor. They may even say, "Thank God, it's Friday." The weekend is "set apart" for breaks in the rhythm of labor. People seek the special time of the party or the happy hour. They celebrate their own special days such as birthdays or wedding anniversaries. They seek relief from the here and now. But these celebrations are markedly different from the sacred time Christians celebrate. Eliade remarks at length about this:

> For religious man, on the contrary, profane temporal duration can be periodically arrested; for certain rituals have the power to interrupt it by periods of a sacred time that is nonhistorical (in the sense that it does not belong to the historical present). Just as a church constitutes a break in plane in the profane space of a modern city, the service celebrated inside it marks a break in profane temporal duration. It is no longer today's historical time that is present—but the time in which the historical existence of Jesus Christ occurred, the time sanctified by his preaching, by his passion, death, and resurrection.[4]

Each Sabbath day, believers observe sacred time in the context of worship. It is the keeping holy of the Sabbath day that marks the regular sacred time for the Christian. The worship service is a marking of a special liturgical time. Because of the reality of the Incarnation, history itself becomes sacred for the Christian. We mark our calendars with reference to time that is B.C. or A.D. We have a theology of history because we realize that there is a holy purpose to history, even our salvation.

In the Old Testament the chief moment of sacred time is that which marked the remembrance of the Exodus from Egypt and the Passover. God instituted an annual feast to celebrate this act of redemption:

> This is a day you are to commemorate; for the generations to come you shall celebrate it as a festival to the LORD—a lasting ordinance. For seven days you are to eat bread made without yeast. On the first day remove the yeast from your houses, for whoever eats anything with yeast in it from the first day through the seventh must be cut off from Israel. On the first day hold a sacred assembly, and another one on the seventh day. Do no work at all on these days, except to prepare food for everyone to eat—that is all you may do.

> Celebrate the Feast of Unleavened Bread, because it was on this very day that I brought your divisions out of Egypt. Celebrate this day as a lasting ordinance for the generations to come. (Exod. 12:14-17)

Similarly, the New Testament sees the replacing of the Passover celebration by the commemoration of the Lord's Supper. The sacrament of the Lord's Supper was first instituted by Christ in the context of the celebration of the Passover. During the Passover meal, Jesus changed the significance of the liturgy as part of the institution of the New Covenant, wherein the elements that were formerly used to recall the Exodus now are used to express the supreme Exodus that would be accomplished by His death on the cross:

> While they were eating, Jesus took bread, gave thanks and broke it, and gave it to his disciples, saying, "Take and eat; this is my body."
>
> Then he took the cup, gave thanks and offered it to them, saying, "Drink from it, all of you. This is my blood of the covenant, which is poured out for many for the forgiveness of sins. I tell you, I will not drink of this fruit of the vine from now on until that day when I drink it anew with you in my Father's kingdom." (Matt. 26:26-29)

The celebration of the Lord's Supper involves sacred time in three distinct ways. First, it looks to the past, instructing believers to remember and to show forth Christ's death by this observance. Second, it focuses on the present moment of celebration, in which Christ meets with His people to nurture them and strengthen them in their sanctification. Third, it looks to the future, to the certain hope of their reunion with Christ in heaven, where they will participate in the banquet feast of the Lamb and His bride.

In sacred space and sacred time Christians find the presence of the holy. The bars that seek to shut out the transcendent are shattered, and the present time becomes defined by the intrusion of the holy. When we erect barriers to these intrusions, dikes to keep them from flooding our souls, we exchange the holy for the profane and rob both God of His glory and ourselves of His grace.

Soli Deo gloria.

Allowing God's Holiness to Touch Our Lives

As you reflect about what you have learned and redis-covered about God's holiness, answer these questions. Use a journal to record your responses to God's holi-ness, or discuss your responses with a friend.

1. Where have you experienced a sense of threshold, of sacred space?
2. In what ways have you looked for a doorway to holy space? Do you go to a specific place—in your home, in your church, in nature—to feel closer to God?
3. What holy times can you pinpoint in your life?
4. How can you cultivate the sense of God's presence and holiness in your life?

Glory to the Holy One

R. C. Sproul

Stuart Sacks
1991

Maestoso con moto
Introduction

2 Tpts.
Hm.

Trb.
Tuba

(A, D, E)*

Cymbals
Timpani

1. Seat - ed on the e - ther throne, A - bove all mor - tal view; The
2. All a - round the mer - cy seat The wing - ed crea - tures sang;
3. shield - ed eyes and cov - ered feet, The an - gels hov - ered high, While
4. Woe is me, the crea - ture wailed, His face u - pon the floor, With

King su - preme in glo - ry sat, Bathed in re - ful - gent hue;
Glo - ry to our God on high, Their poig - nant an - them rang;
glo - ry shook the por - tal walls, And smoke rose to the sky.
dir - ty lips and loath - some tongue His heart could stand no more.

* if only 2 Timps tune to A & D; play notes in parenthesis

Ho - ly, ho - ly, ho - ly, cried the ser - aph throng;

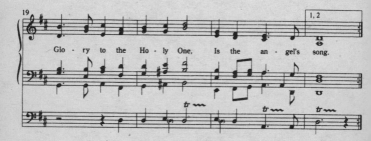

Glo - ry to the Ho - ly One, Is the an - gel's song.

Interlude

song. 3. With song. *sfz*

(Bb, Eb, F)**

meno mosso

allargando 5. Come, an - gel quick and

mf *ff*

** if only 2 timps, tune to Bb, Eb; play notes in parenthesis

purge my lips, Make pure my soul a - new;_____ And
I shall rise and stand a - gain, And I will go for You._____
Ho - ly, ho - ly, ho - ly, ho - ly, cried the ser - aph throng;_____

cymbals

poco rall.

Glo - ry to the Ho - ly One, Is the an - gel's song.

NOTES

CHAPTER 3—THE FEARFUL MYSTERY

1. Rudolf Otto, *The Idea of the Holy* (Oxford: Oxford University Press, 1950), 12–13.

CHAPTER 5—THE INSANITY OF LUTHER

1. Martin Luther, *The Bondage of the Will*, trans. J. I. Packer and O. R. Johnson (Old Tappan, N.J.: Revell, 1970), 63.
2. Roland Bainton, *Here I Stand* (Nashville: Abingdon, 1950), 15.
3. Ibid., 30.
4. Ibid., 64.
5. Ibid., 139.
6. Ewald M. Plass, ed., *What Luther Says* (St. Louis: Concordia, 1959), 1107–8.
7. Bainton, *Here I Stand*, 144.
8. Ibid.
9. Ibid., 34.
10. Ibid., 41.
11. Ibid., 42.
12. Ibid., 43.
13. Ibid., 50.

CHAPTER 9—GOD IN THE HANDS OF ANGRY SINNERS

1. *The Works of Jonathan Edwards, vol. II* (Carlisle, Penn.: Banner of Truth, 1974), 10.
2. Ibid., 9.
3. Ibid., 8.

CHAPTER 10—LOOKING BEYOND SHADOWS

1. John Calvin, *The Institutes of the Christian Religion, vol. I,*
   trans. Henry Beveridge (Grand Rapids: Eerdmans, 1964), 57.

CHAPTER 11—HOLY SPACE AND HOLY TIME

1. Mircea Eliade, *The Sacred and the Profane* (New York:
   Harper & Row, 1961), 23.
2. Ibid., 26.
3. Ibid.
4. Ibid., 72.

LIGONIER MINISTRIES

Renew your Mind.

We're dedicated to helping Christians know what they believe, why they believe it, how to live it, and how to share it.

In order to grow, we need wise instruction from the mind of God about how to think and what we should think about. God calls us to be transformed by His Spirit rather than conformed to the pattern of thinking in this world. And the way of transformation is through the renewing of our minds. It's our goal to proclaim God's holiness, teach His Word with clarity, and see lives changed as we dig deeper into the rich soil of God's truth.

In 1971, as it is today, the world was filled with challenges to biblical faith. Christians who sought to be equipped to answer these challenges had few options short of going to seminary. R.C. Sproul saw the need to offer a bridge of learning for the growing Christian but in a way that was accessible and practical, and Ligonier Ministries was born.

Our educational mission continues today through our books, monthly magazine, broadcasts, conferences, teaching series, music, and website. The appetite for these materials continues to grow both domestically and internationally. We believe that when the Bible is taught clearly, God is seen in all of His majesty and holiness — hearts are conquered, minds are renewed, communities are transformed.

Our hope is for Ligonier Ministries to become a trusted resource to help stimulate Gospel conviction and courage. We are excited about the future because we serve a great and sovereign God. And we know what we are called to do.

FOR MORE INFORMATION,
PLEASE VISIT WWW.LIGONIER.ORG
OR CALL 800-435-4343.

man in the mirror

Our mission is to help every church disciple every man.
We equip leaders with tools to help men grow closer to Christ.

Check out our **bookstore** to find books by Patrick Morley, including
*Man in the Mirror, Devotions for Couples, A Man's Guide to the Spiritual
Disciplines, No Man Left Behind,* and much more!

Take a look at our CD and DVD Bible study series including *10 Questions
that Trouble Every Thinking Man, Biblical Manhood, Twelve Tasks of an
Effective Father,* and many others!

Always on the go? Study the Bible online with Patrick Morley. Get the
thirty-five-minute studies available for free 24/7. Available in both
webcast, audio/video downloads and even podcasts!

You can find all these great resources and more online at
www.maninthemirror.org.
Or you may call us at **1-800-929-2536** or
407-472-2100 for more information.

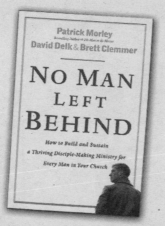